GOD INCOGNITO

*"There is only one way
for believers to bring God to
the men of our time, and
that is to share their
human ideal, and to search
at their side for the God
whom we already possess
but who is present among us
yet as if we did not
recognize him."*

Pierre Teilhard de Chardin

GOD INCOGNITO

S. PAUL SCHILLING

ABINGDON PRESS • NASHVILLE AND NEW YORK

Library of Congress Cataloging in Publication Data

SCHILLING, SYLVESTER PAUL, 1904-   . God incognito.
Includes bibliographical references. 1. God. 2. Experi-
ence. (Religion) I. Title.
BT102.S33   211   73-12756

ISBN 0-687-15133-3

MANUFACTURED BY THE PARTHENON PRESS AT
NASHVILLE, TENNESSEE, UNITED STATES OF AMERICA

PREFACE

In *God in an Age of Atheism* (Abingdon Press, 1969) I examined some major forms of Western atheistic humanism in the nineteenth and twentieth centuries, then attempted to rethink the meaning of God in the light of the atheistic critique. There are today large numbers of serious persons who are committed to high human values, but explicitly or implicitly deny all belief in a more-than-human God. Listening to the objections of some of them, as expressed in both personal conversation and published writings, proved to be a valuable learning experience.

From a critical analysis of the chief bases of unbelief several constructive proposals emerged. These sought to modify traditional conceptions of God by removing weaknesses and errors, to bring to light truths sometimes obscured, and to elucidate certain emphases especially needed today. In the light of these proposals, the closing chapter suggested that though the meaning of God always eludes complete comprehension by finite minds, it may be expressed most intelligibly in terms of four conceptual models taken together: being, dynamic process, love, and personal life. We may thus think of God as the dynamic personal love at the heart of reality; as the creative, energizing actuality of the personal life which in love animates and interpenetrates all that is and seeks ever to realize new dimensions of value; or as the active, ultimate ground of all being and becoming, superlatively personal and good, who is supremely manifest in Jesus Christ.

Such an understanding, I believe, has much to commend it. Yet if this be granted, a further question arises immediately. Can God so interpreted be actually experienced? The conceptualization may be defensible, but does it correspond to anything encounterable in real life? The view of divine reality presented was built up in close relation to human experience, not in an ivory tower. Nevertheless, it still needs to be tested in relation to the day-by-day lives of serious-minded people. Is there evidence that human beings can and do enter into genuine relationshps of trust, worship, and commitment with God conceived in the fourfold manner outlined?

The present book is an endeavor to answer questions like these. At the very start, however, the effort faces the hard fact that for many people today God however conceived is hidden or absent. To them he does not make himself known, and their searches lead to no conscious disclosure of his presence. At the same time, in a wide variety of previously unexpected quarters one finds repeated references to pervasive activities which transcend both individuals and society as a whole, and which women and men do not produce or fashion according to their wishes, but confront. This wide recognition of transcendent reality suggests that what is involved may be the actual presence of God, as it were, incognito.

Is it possible that in our time God may be acting in creative and liberating ways in experiences which for various reasons are not recognized by those who have them as experiences of the divine? There is a good deal of evidence—in the works of contemporary psychologists, sociologists, artists, novelists, and poets, and in the data of ordinary life accessible to all thoughtful persons

—that this is true. The pages that follow explore that possibility. Religious experience in the historical sense, entailing conscious awareness of the divine, is taken with the continued seriousness that it merits. However, special attention is devoted to a variety of broader experiences which point toward a transcendent dimension not ordinarily identified as God. This exploration of possible divine incognitos represents a partial shift from the original intention of the study, but one that I hope may prove as fruitful to the reader as it has been for the writer.

During the gathering and organization of data as well as the writing itself I have profited from seminar discussions and informal conversations with theological students and faculty colleagues at Wesley Theological Seminary, Washington, D.C., and earlier at Boston University and Union Theological Seminary, Dasmariñas, Philippines. They have aided considerably in the formulation, sharpening, and modification of ideas. I am especially indebted to Prof. John D. Godsey, esteemed friend and co-worker in systematic theology at Wesley, who has read the entire manuscript and offered valuable critical comments. The personal interest and constructive suggestions of Paul E. Johnson, cherished longtime friend and colleague at Boston University, have been singularly helpful.

Thanks are due most of all to my wife, who has typed the manuscript, including some revisions, with painstaking care; suggested clarifying changes in style and content; assisted in proofreading and indexing; and given her unfailing encouragement.

S. Paul Schilling

Washington, D.C.
March 19, 1973

CONTENTS

PART THREE: THE COGNITIVE VALUE OF RELIGIOUS EXPERIENCE

PART

1

GOD ABSENT AND PRESENT

1 THE MISSING STAR

Y ou will arrive alone, on a lost shore, where a star will descend on your baggages of sand." So writes André Breton in a poem which suggests the title of Anna Langfus's novel, *The Lost Shore*. A reviewer of the book comments, "The loneliness is here, and the barren shore, and the unsubstantial baggages, but the star is missing." [1] These words reflect accurately not only the purposelessness of the central character in the novel, but also the outlook of multitudes of flesh-and-blood people today, for whom the light of faith in anything other than man himself has gone out—or has never been kindled.

When Nietzsche's now-familiar madman appeared in the marketplace with his lantern at midday to proclaim the death of God, he admitted that men were not ready to fathom or accept so earth-shaking an event. A century later, however, the cold night of the absence of God has become for many in the Western world a numbing—or liberating—reality. God may be lamented, wistfully longed for, happily discarded, or even verbally affirmed, but evidence multiplies that personal awareness of his presence has grown dim. We live in a time of the divine hiddenness. Whatever may

[1] Anna Balakian in the *Saturday Review*, January 25, 1964, p. 38.

be real behind the clouds, what is experienced by many—even by some who are sincere seekers—is not cosmic illumination or support, but silent, unresponsive darkness.

Recognition of this situation is imperative for all who would understand the contemporary status of religious faith. However, it should be balanced by an equally clear-sighted acknowledgment of two other circumstances. One is the fact that in the Hebrew-Christian tradition the actions and intentions of God have frequently been experienced as veiled even to those who trust him. The exclamation of Second Isaiah is fairly typical: "Truly, thou art a God who hidest thyself" (Isa. 45:15). Repeatedly the Psalmist cries, "Why dost thou hide thyself in times of trouble?" "How long wilt thou hide thy face from me?" (Pss. 10:1; 13:1; cf. 44: 24; 88:14). Job charges that God has not only hidden his face, but that he has cruelly persecuted Job, taken away his right, and treated him like an enemy. Bitterly he laments, "Oh, that I knew where I might find him" (Job 23:3; 13:24; 30:21; 27:2). The recurrence of such experiences moved Pascal to declare that no religion which fails to assert the hiddenness of God can be regarded as true.

God is so transcendent, insists Rudolf Bultmann, that we can believe him "only in spite of experience, just as we can accept justification only in spite of conscience." [2] From a very different orientation H. D. Lewis emphasizes that, in view of the divine transcendence, "the only thing in particular which is precluded for a finite creature is to have that unmediated contact with God which reduces the absolute mystery of His essential nature." [3] Yet the God who is veiled in mystery, and who may even conceal himself, is also the God who acts in manifold ways to disclose

---

[2] *Jesus Christ and Mythology* (New York: Charles Scribner's Sons, 1958), p. 84.
[3] *Our Experience of God* (New York: The Macmillan Co., 1959), p. 284.

himself to men. For historic Hebrew and Christian faith God is both *absconditus* and *revelatus,* hidden as well as revealed.

The second circumstance demanding attention is unmistakable evidence today of heightened and increasing interest in the exploration of the transcendent in human life, coupled with recurring reports of experiences ascribed by those who have them to divine activity. The wide popularity of the musicals "Jesus Christ, Superstar" and "Godspell," especially the long runs of the stage versions of the latter, indicate a real openness to the gospel message when it is freed from the accretions of traditional sanctity and expressed in the idioms of today. The hymn "Amazing Grace" has become a favorite of rock singers and a best seller in the record shops. Many youth who previously were "turned off" by anything resembling religion have in the early seventies joined the ranks of the "Jesus people." The charismatic or neo-Pentecostal movement within a number of mainstream Christian communions, especially the Roman Catholic, has also been winning increasing numbers of participants, among whom a personal experience of the Holy Spirit is the dominant concern. Any easy assumption that unbelief is the wave of the future is also belied by the spontaneous emergence in many lands of small religious groups devoted to the search for a deeper spiritual reality than their members have found in traditional organized religion. Particularly significant perhaps are those who seek through adaptations of various Buddhist or Hindu disciplines of transcendental meditation the attainment of *satori* or union with God. Such movements may indicate little more than a deeply felt need for some belief or commitment—in reaction against the glorification in Western culture of impersonal scientific objectivity and detachment. Some of them are impaired by one-sidedness, dogmatic intolerance, uncritical emotionalism, or lack of social concern. Some may be only passing fads, no more indicative of genuine search for the reality of God than soaring current interest in astrology, witchcraft, voodoo, or Satanistic cults. Nevertheless, they are part of the current scene, and they must therefore be included in any sound effort to estimate the present state of man's experience of God. Evidence of a different kind is provided by the recent scholarly work of social scientists like Peter L. Berger, Robert N. Bellah, and Abraham H. Maslow, who are exploring with new seriousness the implications of the "peak experiences" of men and women, their quest for dignity and meaning, their potentialities for personal growth, and the manifold phenomena which may be interpreted as "signals of transcendence." Some of these implications will be explored below.

Yet when all due allowance has been made for the circumstances just sketched, there remains solid basis for the judgment that in recent decades personal theistic faith has eroded to a degree unprecedented in Western history. The total number of persons who can testify to a personal awareness of God is still relatively small. In the winter of 1973 a serious-minded Christian journalist of Silver Spring, Maryland, preparing for a panel discussion of laymen on the experience of God, to be held at Wesley Seminary, asked some of his associates to share with him their questions about God. He reported that the majority of them were surprised that he even raised the question. What relevance, they asked, does such a query have today? The eclipse of God is by no means total, but it is extensive. Statements as sweeping as these by Thomas J. J. Altizer would no doubt command wide support: "Men do not today experience God except as hidden, absent, silent." "The man who chooses to live in our destiny can neither know the reality of God's presence nor understand the world as his creation." [4] For Altizer there remains for "modern man" no transcendent ground, awesome mystery, or ultimate norm for his

---

[4] Thomas J. J. Altizer and William Hamilton, *Radical Theology and the Death of God* (Indianapolis: Bobbs-Merrill, 1966), pp. xi, 95. Cf. *ibid.*, p. 15; Altizer, *Mircea Eliade and the Dialectic of the Sacred* (Philadelphia: The Westminster Press, 1966), p. 22.

life, and this means liberation from the alien power of the deity formerly believed in. William Hamilton declares, "We do not adore, do not possess, do not believe in God. . . . We are not talking about the absence of the experience of God, but about the experience of the absence of God." [5]

Even in the churches—some observers would say, *especially* there—one finds little evidence of that direct, firsthand, life-transforming consciousness of God which the churches presumably exist to encourage. Methodists, for example, continue to laud John Wesley for his "strange warming of the heart" at Aldersgate, but few indeed have known such an experience themselves, and few could testify to that personal witness of the Spirit which he believed possible for every Christian. Surely it is ironic that, after a generation in which theologians have proclaimed most eloquently, in myriads of books, the importance of an I-Thou encounter between man and God, and when such a meeting has come to be widely regarded as normative for Christian faith, there are so few for whom it is an existential reality.

Partly as a result of this situation, and doubtless partly responsible for it, is the decline in meaning of public worship, in which the traditional elements of scripture, sermon, sacrament, hymn, and prayer have become for many empty formalities. Moreover, many theological students today are motivated not by personal faith in a God who has called them to ministry, but mainly by high-minded humanistic concern to advance justice and love in society, and they are quite vague as to how this concern may be related to any extra-human or ultimate ground. Clearly any genuine personal experience of the presence of God today is both difficult and rare.

It is much easier to describe a development of this kind than to account for it. The causes of the recent decline in religious

[5] "The Death-of-God Theology," *The Christian Scholar,* 48 (1965), 31.

faith are varied and complex, and no simple explanation is possible. Among many factors which would merit attention, three may be mentioned here.

1. Of primary significance, perhaps, is the multi-faceted influence of contemporary culture, which powerfully affects men's self-understanding and their apprehension of ultimate meanings. At least three interwoven strands of this influence can be identified.

a. Modern life is marked by rapid and extensive change. As a result of unprecedented scientific advances, the material conditions of existence for hundreds of millions of people have altered more in the past few decades than in many centuries. The impact of two world wars, many regional conflicts, and repeated social and political revolutions has swiftly and irrevocably changed the character of society and undermined many time-honored customs and institutions. However, change typically increases uncertainty, doubt, and apprehension. This is likely to be especially true with reference to religious attitudes, beliefs, and practices, which are peculiarly dependent on particular historical events and the meanings which have come to be assigned to them. When the continuity of the present with the past is broken, the process of readjustment and reinterpretation inevitably becomes threatening to all cherished values, especially when the styles and conditions of life are not only novel but themselves unstable. The relevance of insights and convictions inherited from the remote past to the complex demands of the present moment and the impinging future is not readily apparent. Even the language of religious experience seems alien to the new situation, and the problem of translation is a formidable one. As a result, the content of once-cherished beliefs along with the ambiguous forms in which they are expressed is called into question and often jettisoned as excess baggage.

b. Also contributory to the loss of a sense of immediacy in religion today is the pluralism of modern life. In the United States, for example, the relatively homogeneous culture of an earlier period has given way to great diversity, with a wide variety of value claims, world views, and life styles bidding for attention and allegiance. In the marketplace of competing ideas many persons inevitably become less certain of the adequacy and superiority of their own. In this situation the secure, comfortable acceptance of a faith once widely held by a supportive majority is rendered impossible.

c. Closely related to the two influences just mentioned, and probably more determinative than either, is the all-pervasive effect of modern science and technology. The substantial values which have accrued to mankind through the bold and painstaking investigations of men of science are everywhere recognized. The method followed by the natural sciences, which moves from empirical observation through hypothesis and controlled experiment to verification and the formulation of laws commanding universal assent, has vastly increased man's knowledge of his world. The technological application of this constantly expanding knowledge has given man unprecedented control over nature, reduced drastically the amount of labor needed to sustain his existence, and made possible the improvement of the quality of his life.

Nevertheless, science and technology have lent strong support to the mechanization and depersonalization of human life. The demonstrated results of scientific method have lent an authority to the rigorously objective and detached approach associated with science, and consequently exposed to suspicion the personal interests and involvements of human beings, that can be readily dismissed as merely subjective. If the approved road to knowledge is the kind of experimental investigation which seeks to discover and express in exact formulas the uniformities of objective reality, those aspects of human life that cannot be investigated in this way can be granted at best only a second-class citizenship in the community of truth-seekers. The aesthetic, ethical, and religious experiences of men and women are then significant only for the individuals who have them.

For this diminution of our total humanity there is no warrant in science itself, which if true to its basic attitude should be open to all empirical data. However, the cult of scientific objectivity, claiming the support of the scientific enterprise itself, has won many adherents, and it exerts wide influence today. "As a whole generation of men," writes R. D. Laing, "we are so estranged from the inner world that there are many arguing that it does not exist; and that even if it does exist, it does not matter." [6] It is widely assumed that the really important things and ideas are those which can be precisely measured, or which yield tangible results in making man's life more comfortable, convenient, or enjoyable. This assumption leads unavoidably to a decline in spiritual sensitivity, whether to other persons, animal life, physical nature as seen by poet and artist, or that ultimate ground of our existence which men have called God.

2. A second cause of the decline in personal awareness of the divine may be found in the secularizing process which has marked recent interpretations of the Christian faith itself—although this has been significantly affected by broad sociological tendencies.

Here the analysis of Thomas Luckmann is instructive. He points out that in archaic societies and traditional civilizations the whole of individual and social life was embraced in a kind of sacred cosmos. Such institutions as kinship, the division of labor, and

[6] *The Politics of Experience and the Bird of Paradise* (New York: Ballantine Books, [1967] 1970), p. 46.

the exercise and control of power were pervaded by religious representations which bound them into an indissoluble unity of meaning. Hence no activity could be adequately understood without reference to religion. In modern industrial society this unity was largely replaced by a segmentation of the social structure into various institutional domains, each exercising considerable autonomy. Religious institutions, like others, became increasingly more specialized in their functions and more restricted in their jurisdiction. For a variety of reasons, in Western Christianity more than anywhere else religion became subject to institutional specialization. The traditional sacred cosmos was compressed into one segment of life, and religion became largely autonomous and divorced from the other institutions of society. Certain beliefs and patterns of behavior came to be regarded as specifically religious, with normative expectations officially defined and interpreted. In recent years, however, institutionally specialized religion has waned. Instead of one official model of religion, several "ex-official" models vie with one another and with systems of knowledge and value such as economics and politics which lack any specifically religious orientation. In this situation the individual may adopt a neutral or indifferent attitude toward the model of religion formerly determinative in his tradition, no longer finding it helpful in the interpretation of his life. He may then go on to construct from diverse sources his own private system of religious beliefs.[7]

In two respects this analysis of Thomas Luckmann helps us to understand the current decline in religious sensitivity. First, when the individual exercises considerable freedom in building his own religion, he may feel less secure and less sure of the object of his worship than when his views are supported by the whole structure

[7] "Belief, Unbelief, and Religion," *The Culture of Unbelief,* ed. Rocco Caporale and Antonio Grumelli (Berkeley: University of California Press, 1971), pp. 21-37.

of a unified society or by the authority of an institutional church. Secondly, since his religion is less determined by the specialized institution which encouraged him to treat it as a separate domain, it seems likely to function more in interrelation with other overlapping areas of his total experience.

This second possibility deserves special consideration. Here Luckmann's investigations provide an illuminating sociological background for the theology of secularization or "worldly Christianity" associated with Dietrich Bonhoeffer, Hans Hoekendijk, Harvey Cox, and others, the central intent of which finds wide support today among both Catholics and Protestants. Thoughtful Christians now decisively reject the dualism of sacred and profane, holy and secular. God is seen as creatively and redemptively at work in all aspects of human existence, hence religious faith has to do with the whole of life. Yet there is evidence, however unexpected, that this very holistic conception of religion may affect negatively the personal apprehension of the divine presence which traditional Christianity has regarded as normative.

Is it possible that this kind of experience of God is more likely when religion is separated from the rest of life as a specialized area cultivated by the churches, and when God is sought particularly through the specifically "religious" practices which are officially recommended? If so, the more religion is seen as an isolated segment, the more the individual will be psychologically prepared for a feeling-awareness of God regarded as authentic precisely because it is sharply distinguished from other experiences. Conversely, the more God is seen as interpenetrating the whole of nature and history, the broader and less intense will be the sense of his reality. Then the personal consciousness of God may be expected to diminish as the segmentation of religion breaks down and the wholeness of life is restored. It should then occasion no surprise if the belief that the whole world is the sphere of God's action is accompanied by a decline in the vividness of men's emotional sense of his presence. If the transcendent in its fullness is located in the ordinary, it is less likely to be perceived with special power in the exceptional.[8] God himself may be no less real, but men will be less conscious of him than if they related him still to the old, more restricted frame of reference.

3. A further cause of men's failure to discern the presence of God today is their practical immersion in other more limited concerns. This may take various forms. It may involve such an absorption in the search for economic well-being, material success, and ego-fulfillment that there is little time or energy for the pursuit of higher values. We may place ourselves and our selfish goals so solidly in the middle that no room remains for our true Center. Man-made idols get in the way of the only worthy Ultimate. A transforming experience became possible for Moses when he resolved, "I will turn aside and see this great sight, why the bush is not burnt" (Exod. 3:1-6). But multitudes are too inattentive to recognize the nearness of the divine or too busy to turn aside to look. Spiritual sensitivity is not accidental; it must be nourished by times of reflection on life's meaning and openness to realities greater than our own.

Sometimes the difficulty lies in a distorted conception of God and what service to him entails—even on the part of professed believers and worshipers. One of the characters in Ignazio Silone's novel *Bread and Wine* boasts of the accomplishments of his parish—and his own—in a passage which might apply to innumerable Christian congregations:

[8] "The presence of Christ in the Blessed Sacrament is threatened in its unique character by the argument that Christ is also present in his word, in our neighbor and the Church." (Irene Marinoff, "The Erosion of the Mystery," *New Theology No. 7,* ed. Martin E. Marty and Dean G. Peerman [New York: The Macmillan Co., 1970], p. 28.)

"In my parish in these last years, enormous spiritual progress has been made, thanks be to God," he said. "Enormous!" he repeated with emphasis. "The number of confessions has gone up by forty per cent and the communions by thirty. Even if I do say so myself, I don't know what parish can beat that." [9]

When "spiritual progress" is so radically misconstrued, the true life of the Spirit dies of malnutrition.

Sometimes the decisive factor is simply human self-assurance, the confidence that man is quite capable of handling his own affairs. This is a kind of practical counterpart of the exaggerated belief in the power of modern technology, previously mentioned. Donald Hughes's parody on the familiar hymn of Isaac Watts expresses strikingly a mood which is still widespread in spite of the collapse of many of men's fondest hopes:

> O God our help in ages past
> (Or so the Psalmist said),
> We now can face the stormy blast
> Without external aid.[10]

In ways like these, the hiddenness of God in our time is often due to the action or inaction of men themselves. Like the young Augustine, we have simply turned our backs to the light.

Though the three types of influence discussed above do not pretend to be an exhaustive listing of the major grounds of the dimness of modern man's awareness of God, they may be taken as fairly representative. However they are weighted in relation to one another, and regardless of whether theoretical or practical considerations are regarded as more decisive, together they have produced a serious, perhaps unprecedented, disintegration of personal religious faith.

In Silone's moving story the old priest Don Benedetto, pained

[9] (New York: *Athenaeum,* [1946] 1962), p. 26.
[10] "Neo-Matins," *Prism,* May, 1964.

by the inhumanity of Fascist Italy's invasion of Ethiopia, admits that he has sometimes asked himself, "Where is God and why has He abandoned us?" [11] The form of words varies widely, but the same basic question confronts many sensitive, serious-minded persons in today's world. Can God still be experienced? If so, how? Where is he at work? What does the term *God* itself mean? Are we now restricted wholly to immanence, or is it possible to have authentic contact with some transcendent reality? In a time when for so many God is absent, can we still speak of him as really present, active in human life here and now? Such questions are the central concern of this book.

Both the infrequency of immediate experiences of God and the causes cited suggest the desirability of a broadened concept of what constitutes authentic religious experience. It is, of course, quite possible to infer from the present situation, as some have done, that God is dead or has never lived. But a defensible and possibly a sounder alternative would be to redefine what it means to experience the divine presence.

Historically, a specialized understanding has been dominant. In Christian biography, for example, accounts of the experience of God tend to regard as normative vivid personal events like Paul's transforming vision on the Damascus road; Augustine's hearing of the voice, "Take up and read," in Ambrose's monastery garden in Milan, and his inner perception of the light which swept the darkness of doubt from his heart; and Wesley's "strange warming of the heart" at a prayer meeting on Aldersgate Street, London.

Similarly, highly influential interpretations of religious experience have accentuated the immediacy and emotional quality of the occurrence. John Wesley writes that we know by direct assurance or an "immediate consciousness" if our souls are alive to God. The true Christian believer has "a sure trust and confidence in

---

[11] *Bread and Wine*, p. 275.

God, that, through the merits of Christ, his sins are forgiven, and he reconciled to the favour of God." He is given "the testimony of the Spirit," "an inward impression on the soul, whereby the Spirit of God immediately and directly witnesses to [his] spirit, that [he is] a child of God." [12] For Schleiermacher religion is centrally a feeling of absolute dependence. Though William James's formal definition of religion is broad enough to include "the feelings, acts, and experiences of individual men in their solitude," in relation to what they consider the divine, religion as he presents it in his *Varieties of Religious Experience* is characteristically "enthusiasm in solemn emotion." Most of his attention is directed to "the deliverances of direct religious experience," "the extremer expressions of the religious temperament," under such topics as the sick soul, the divided self and its unification, conversion, saintliness, and mysticism.[13] Rudolf Otto associates "the holy" with man's sense of the numinous, the creature-feeling aroused by his consciousness of being in the presence of the *mysterium tremendum,* the Wholly Other which awes and overpowers him but also grips him with an uncanny fascination.[14]

This understanding of religious experience deserves the prominent place it has held in the classical literature on the subject. The intensity of the direct apprehension of God has varied considerably in different periods, being more pronounced apparently in such movements as the evangelical revivals in England in the eighteenth century and in America in the late nineteenth and early twentieth centuries. But evidence of its persistence through the centuries is abundant, as for example in Christian

[12] Sermons: "The Witness of the Spirit: I," I, 5-7; "The Marks of the New Birth," I, 2-5; "The Witness of the Spirit: II," II, 2-4.

[13] (New York: Longmans, Green, and Co., [1902] 1925), pp. vi-x, 31, 48, 455, 486, 501.

[14] *The Idea of the Holy* (London: Humphrey Milford, Oxford University Press, 1928), pp. 1-40 and *passim.*

hymnody. Nevertheless, it would be misleading to conclude that genuine faith in God exists, or that God himself is present, only when there is an immediate personal consciousness of his presence. The fact that even John Wesley described the warming of his heart as "strange" suggests the possible authenticity of other manifestations of the divine reality. Many Christians today would have difficulty in matching the fervor of Fanny Crosby in singing, "Blessed assurance, Jesus is mine"; yet this provides no warrant for dismissing their faith as spurious. As Karl Rahner has suggested, some persons are apparently "unmusical in religion"—temperamentally incapable of experiencing the full range of its potential meaning. As we have seen, a variety of social and cultural factors may also dim religious awareness. By contrast, some intensely emotional experiences regarded unquestioningly by those who have them as experiences of God may be little more than vivid states of consciousness with no correspondingly objective reality whatever.

Considerations like these indicate that the relation between God and man covers a much wider range of human experience than has conventionally been imagined. There may be many events in which men and women enter into real contact with the living God even though they are not conscious of his presence and may not interpret as divine the reality which they encounter. If this is true, we are compelled to ask afresh, What is it then which constitutes an experience of God? What kinds of occurrences should be so characterized? More broadly, what is the basic meaning of religious experience?

2 EXPERIENCE AND RELIGIOUS EXPERIENCE

T he meaning of the English word experience is illuminated
by its etymology. It is derived from the Latin *experiens,* the
present participle of the verb *experiri,* to try, test, or prove. The
infinitive *experiri* is in turn a combination of the prefix *ex,* out, and
the root of *peritus,* skilled, experienced. Closely related to this
Latin root are the Greek *peros,* a way through; *pereuein,* to convey;
pereuesthai, to go, march; and *peran,* to pass through. Traceable
to such Greek origins, by way of the Anglo-Saxon *faran,* are
such modern cognates as the Dutch *varen,* the German *fahren,* and
the English *fare,* all meaning to travel, go, or journey. Further
light is shed if we compare the word experience with the English
peril, which is derived from a term akin to *peritus*—the Latin noun
periculum or *periclum,* trial, test, danger.

In short, when seen in the light of its origins, to experience
means to try out something by passing or living through it oneself,
with the strong implication that such testing may entail moving
through new and possibly dangerous territory. Experience, then,
is the process of actually living through or undergoing an event
or events. Experience in the fullest sense seems clearly to imply
consciousness, especially if it involves the kind of trying out

which enlarges life or extends one's contact with reality. It is true that a person may undergo certain occurrences without being aware of them, for example, an increase in bodily temperature during sleep, the removal of an appendix during anesthesia, or the painless sustaining of a deep cut during the momentary shock of an accident. However, even such "experiences" are not complete until the subject becomes aware, after the unconscious event, of the discomfort of the fever, the abdominal incision, or the open wound.

It should also be recognized that experience is not limited to one particular form of conscious life, such as feeling or sense perception. It embraces all the processes of consciousness, cognitive and volitional no less than emotional. Moreover, it includes distorted as well as accurate perception, erroneous as well as correct thinking, hate as well as love, selfish as well as other-regarding choices, encounters with cosmic reality as well as narrowly circumscribed forms of existence, and the impact of imaginary essences as well as of actual entities. With experience not even the sky is the limit.

Given in ordinary experience is our awareness of being in relation to some reality other than our own. The experiencer is an agent, but he is conscious likewise of being acted on by something which he cannot control and which does not depend on him for its existence. Without being able to explain how, he finds himself interpreting the data of his experience as constituting an objective material, social, and axiological environment. In experience, writes John E. Smith, "we *find* something already there, we *come up against* something, we confront persons, objects, events, and we do so with the sense that we *undergo* or receive whatever it is that we meet without any sense of being responsible for having produced it." [1]

[1] *Experience and God* (New York: Oxford University Press, 1968), p. 13.

True, not all the data of consciousness are of this kind, but the normal person is able to discriminate between the purely internal products of his own imagination and the experiences which present themselves as arising from, and referring to, a world external to him, but in which he is integrally involved. Experience as it occurs entails neither a sharp separation between subject and object nor a claim to the superior or sole reality of either, but the assumption that the experiencer sustains an interacting relationship with the world experienced. He may misinterpret, both theoretically and practically, the nature of that world, but he is aware of himself as belonging to it, and one of his major tasks is to discover as far as possible what it is, and what his responsibility is with regard to it.

Religious Experience and Experience of God

If, then, experience is the totality of those processes which the individual lives through in relating himself to his environing world, what do we mean by religious experience? In general, an experience is distinguished as religious not by its peculiar content, but by the way in which it is interpreted or taken by the one who has it. Broadly defined, religion is a person's total relation to whatever he regards as supremely worthy of his trust, devotion, or worship. It is man's attitude toward that which concerns him ultimately. Hence a religious experience may be any experience of any person which he refers to the object of his ultimate commitment. Theistically understood, it is any experience taken or apprehended by the human subject in its relation to his God.

Clearly this judgment implies that some persons may interpret nonreligiously or even atheistically events which for others indicate the presence of God. Both atheists and theists, for example, have noted evidences in nature and history of a dynamic thrust toward the not-yet, promising the coming of the new and offering ground for hope in the possibilities of the future. Christians like Jürgen Moltmann or Karl Rahner ascribe such phenomena to the activity of God, but for the Marxist Ernst Bloch, they are the work of matter (cf. *mater,* mother), itself the creative source of an advancing, open-ended process. Thus the same objective data may provide bases for very different readings of their meaning. The contrast appears vividly in a passage from William Blake: " 'What,' it will be question'd, 'When the Sun rises, do you not see a round disk of fire somewhat like a guinea?' O no, no, I see an Innumerable company of the Heavenly host crying, 'Holy, Holy is the Lord God almighty.' "

The same differences of interpretation arise in relation to content which is conventionally assumed to be religious. The Bible itself may be studied as a collection of various kinds of literature, or as a source of historical information, or in preparation for the production of a movie extravaganza like "Ben Hur" or "The Ten Commandments." It is widely recognized that some of the most "profane" novels and motion pictures have religious subjects. Though the Collect for Purity springs from profoundly religious devotion, its rhythmic words may be spoken by a professor of speech as an example of good diction, without any religious implications whatever. A historian of religion may expound the Hindu doctrine of karma, the Buddhist way of salvation, or the Christian conception of the Trinity as the beliefs of different kinds of religious people, while remaining personally uninvolved and unmoved by any of them, hence without any religious experience of his own.

On the other hand, any event in men's common life may occasion a religious experience if it is related to faith in God. The testimony of the disciples of Jesus, who "was known to them in the breaking of the bread" at Emmaus (Luke 24:35), is echoed in the experience of multitudes of men and women for whom eating and drinking are always occasions for gratitude to God. The

31

painstaking experimentation of a physicist or the patient observations of an ornithologist may be regarded by those who undertake them as ultimately concerned with forms of the creative action of God. For such scientists the search for truth thus becomes a fulfillment of the divine purposes. Charles Munch, one of the great music directors of the Boston Symphony Orchestra, took a similar view of his art. "I regard my conducting," he wrote, "as a sacred vocation, a priesthood; it is not too strong a word."

The recognition that the presence or absence of a religious dimension in experience depends on how it is taken should enable us to avoid two widely held misunderstandings. First, religious experience is not exclusively identifiable with any one form of psychic activity, but involves all aspects and relationships of the personality. Its forms are even more varied than those examined so illuminatingly in William James's classic *Varieties of Religious Experience*. James knew well that the religious life is not restricted to any one special function. For him there are many "really different types of religious experience," and no one essence. He also recognized that the awe, joy, love, and fear which are found in religious experience are psychologically the same emotions which operate in experiences which are not interpreted in religious terms.[2] However, in his *Varieties* he devotes predominant attention to such emotional expressions of religion as sudden conversion and mystical states of consciousness. He declares that his first concern is "to defend . . . 'experience' against 'philosophy' as being the real backbone of the world's religious life—I mean prayer, guidance, and all that sort of thing immediately and privately felt, as against high and noble general views of our destiny and the world's meaning." [3] This aim apparently prevented

---

[2] *Varieties of Religious Experience,* pp. 98, 39, 28.

[3] *The Letters of William James and Theodore Flournoy,* ed. Robert C. Le Clair (Madison, Wis. and London: University of Wisconsin Press, 1966), II, 127.

James from exploring the cognitive and volitional aspects of individual religious experience as well as the corporate dimension of the religious life. The net effect has been support for the conclusions of some interpreters that religion has primarily to do with human feelings.

However, if we are to avoid extreme subjectivism we must recognize that religion is concerned not only with emotion, but with all the activities of the human psyche. As Gordon W. Allport has shown, it has psychological roots as manifold as desire, temperament, values, and search for meaning. It

must be viewed as an indistinguishable blend of emotion and reason, of feeling and meaning. When we study it we are dealing with . . . a posture of the mind in which emotion and logical thinking fuse, . . . a mode of response wherein a combination of feelings is tied to a conception of the nature of things that is thought-provoking, reasonable, and acceptable.[4]

As in all authentic friendship and love of one human being for another, so in the relation of the finite person to God the whole self is involved—intellect and will no less than feeling. Rather than thinking about a religious experience only *after* we have had it, to a greater or less degree we think *while* we are having it. When we enter our closet to pray or the church building to worship with our fellows, we do not check our minds and consciences outside. They are present and active throughout, for we *are* our thinking and willing as well as our feeling. Likewise, the illumination which sometimes comes, though it may be marked more by immediate insight than by discursive reasoning, is genuine only if it is intellectually and morally significant as well as emotionally convincing. Isaiah's vision in the temple involved not only an awesome sense of a mysterious presence, but a new understanding

[4] *The Individual and His Religion* (New York: The Macmillan Co., 1951), pp. 16-17.

of the righteousness of God and a decision to obey the divine will (Isa. 6:6-8).

A second misconception is that which compartmentalizes religious experience by treating it as a special area separated from the rest of life. This view assigns to religion man's experience of the holy or the sacred, a realm which is seen as set apart from aesthetic, moral, scientific, social, economic, and political experience. Rudolf Otto's *Idea of the Holy* is a penetrating and enlightening analysis of the nonrational aspects of religion which he finds focused in the experience of the numinous, blending boundless awe and boundless wonder. He is right in regarding this experience as distinctive in religion. However, in at least two respects Otto's insights need to be complemented. First, religious experience is not confined to man's sense of overwhelming awe and fascination in the presence of the Wholly Other. Secondly, the experience of the numinous, where it does occur, must be related to the whole of our human experience. Perhaps the binding or connecting quality suggested by the Latin root *religio* marks not only the relation of the religious person to his fellow worshipers and his God, but also that between the various aspects of his total experience. If so, John Dewey is right in regarding the religious quality of experience as "the polar opposite of some type of experience that can exist by itself." [5] Instead, it is a quality which may apply to all experience.

Religious experience, as William Temple has declared, is "the whole experience of religious persons." [6] They apprehend God in and through their physical and social environments. As they confront things and people in the day-by-day world they find themselves in the divine presence. They are religious, therefore, not only when they pray or join in public worship, but also when

[5] *A Common Faith* (New Haven: Yale University Press, 1934), pp. 10-11.

[6] *Nature, Man, and God* (London: Macmillan & Co., 1949), p. 334.

they are moved by the glory of a sunset or the harmonies of a concert, when they are re-created by zestful play or a walk in the woods, when through scientific research they learn some new facet of truth, when in relation to their fellows they perceive the path of duty or their failure to follow it, and when the gracious act of a friend speaks to them of the grace of God.

Such experiences may or may not be accompanied by a vivid awareness of God, but for the religious person they are rooted in belief in God and the believer's perceived relationship to him. The man of faith views his environment—though it is approachable from other more partial perspectives—as ultimately suffused with the divine. Thus every aspect of his commerce with it takes on religious meaning.

Religious experience, writes H. Wheeler Robinson, "is not primarily or chiefly a peculiar field of experience in a larger estate; it is rather an intensive culture of common ground." [7] The metaphor is helpful, especially if by *intensive* we keep in mind the intention or intentionality rather than simply the intensity or vigor of the action. Our cultivation of the common life is religious to the degree that it has for us religious meaning, manifesting the reality of God and offering ways for serving him. However, there are also degrees of intensity in such activity, just as there are moments of special intensity in other forms of human awareness. For example, personal prayer ordinarily involves more concentrated attention to and consciousness of one's relation to God than the belief that the world is the creation of God or that history is ultimately subject to divine control. Worship is the point where the pebble strikes the water, while other beliefs and practices are ripples which become less distinct as they move outward. Yet a major element of significance in the more intense forms of reli-

[7] *The Christian Experience of the Holy Spirit* (New York: Harper & Brothers, 1928), p. 59.

gious experience is the fact that they bring to specially clear focus much that is constantly if more marginally apprehended, thereby coloring decisively our whole experience of the world. Light is brightest near the lamp which sheds it, but it pervades the room.

Experience of God in Broader Perspective

In regarding religious experience, with Temple, as "the whole experience of religious persons," we have been thinking primarily of people who themselves perceive their lives as having some ultimate significance, and most of all persons who consciously relate their existence to the reality of God—however they may conceive him. But here a further question arises: What of those men and women who do not think of themselves as religious, and who do not regard the events of their lives as in any way related to God? Is there such a thing as an experience of God which is not apprehended as such by the one who has it? I believe there is.

There are events in which the persons who experience them admittedly find themselves confronting an extra-human dimension that they themselves do not interpret in theistic terms, but which may be legitimately so interpreted by observers who seek to understand the meaning of God in human experience as a whole. Here great care must be exercised to respect the self-images of sincere and thoughtful people, hence to avoid the superficial and arrogant claim that they are believers in spite of themselves. Some of the recurring references to humanitarian atheists and agnostics as "anonymous Christians" illustrate this danger. Nevertheless, if God is real, human beings are in his presence whether they recognize the fact or not, and it is not bigotry for those who regard this as the true situation to state what they think in dialogue with their fellows who exercise their freedom to assert a different conclusion. In this spirit I suggest that there are in human experience intimations of a transcendent reality which are sometimes not taken by those most deeply involved as experiences of God, but which may quite soundly be so interpreted.

The scientific humanist Julian Huxley finds it impossible to explain away experiences like those of an awareness of transcendent power, communion with a higher reality, a sense of sacredness, or a consciousness of inner peace in spite of distress. In Huxley's view such experiences do not involve relations between men and a more-than-human God, but they do point to forces which transcend our private selves, whether in external nature or in our social environment. "They are the outcome of human minds in their strange commerce with outer reality, and in the still stranger and often unconscious internal struggle between their components." [8]

A different kind of recognition of some transsubjective reality appears in a conversation near the end of Ernest Hemingway's novel *The Sun Also Rises*. Brett and Jake are deeply drawn to each other, but cannot marry because Jake was emasculated by a wound in battle. Brett is powerfully attracted to a young Spanish bullfighter, whom she seduces, but she quickly terminates the affair in order to avoid defiling the youth: "I'm not going to be one of those bitches that ruins children." Later she confides in Jake how she feels about her self-denial: "It makes one feel rather good deciding not to be a bitch." When Jake agrees, she adds, "It's sort of what we have instead of God." Then Jake observes, "Some people have God. Quite a lot."

Neither Brett nor Jake has God, and in this they resemble most of Hemingway's other characters. But Jake's courage, Brett's sensitivity to conscience, and the need evident in both for some kind of substitute for God may be responses to something in existence which they do not invent but confront. Their dim awareness of

[8] *Religion Without Relevation,* rev. ed. (New York: Harper & Brothers, [1927] 1957), pp. 44-46, 60, 223.

this inescapable dimension of reality may constitute an authentic experience of God, though quite unrecognized by them for what it is. Similarly, the reality which Huxley and Hamilton experience as the mysterious, the holy, and the transcendent, as well as the interconnectedness which they find in their cosmic and social environments, may be most intelligibly interpreted as the activity of God—whatever terms they may use in describing it.

Are not most serious persons, in their most reflective moments, aware that their pursuit of all the values realizable by human beings occurs in a larger context which intimately and powerfully affects their actions? Often this awareness elicits attitudes of wonder, awe, and dependence; apprehensions of human finitude; and concern to enter into some kind of cooperative relation with an order which manifestly transcends man. The extra-human structure of reality which is encountered in such ways may be soundly regarded as the presence of God, acting, as it were, incognito. In this respect the man of faith, with full respect for those who interpret the data differently, may make his own the words of the final chorus of T. S. Eliot's *Murder in the Cathedral:*

> ... All things exist
> Only in Thy light, and Thy glory is
> declared even in that which denies
> Thee; the darkness declares the
> glory of light.
> Those who deny Thee could not deny,
> if Thou didst not exist; and their
> denial is never complete, for if it
> were so, they would not exist.
> They affirm Thee in living; all things
> affirm Thee in living.

If the foregoing account of religious experience is sound, it is possible to identify three main forms of the experience of God. These may be portrayed as positions on a continuum, as levels, or perhaps most accurately as a series of concentric circles or circular bands. The innermost circle comprises the direct, personal awareness of the divine presence consciously interpreted as such by the experiencer. This may be construed broadly enough to include both the relatively rare instances of mysticism in the classical sense and the less intense consciousness of those who in prayer or corporate worship believe themselves to be in personal communion with God. The second circle includes the entire range of human experiences—physical, intellectual, aesthetic, ethical, social, etc.—when seen by those who have them as manifestations of the divine presence or spheres for the service of God. The outermost circle is made up of a wide variety of intimations of a more-than-human reality, which may not be identified as divine by the persons most directly concerned, but which may nevertheless actually involve the active presence of God. In such cases God may be more hidden than revealed, so that he may perhaps quite properly be regarded as present incognito. No doubt the three forms of experience should be conceived as overlapping somewhat, so that the model of a continuum or spectrum applies even if we think primarily in terms of levels or concentric circles.

The form taken by an individual's experience of God would seem to depend partly on his psychological makeup, partly on the seriousness of his religious concern, and partly on the social and cultural influences which affect him. This suggests that the same person may experience God in different ways at different times. Presumably persons for whom circle one is normative may also regularly find themselves in circle two, and occasionally even in circle three. Those best equipped to experience God in the middle circle may on occasion move toward either the center or the periphery. However, those who for whatever reason are located primarily in circle three may find it exceedingly difficult to move into the innermost circle, though their way to circle two would seem always to remain open.

The extension of the experience of God to include unrecognized intimations of his reality provides no warrant whatever for regarding the other forms of religious experience as unimportant. On the contrary, they furnish the necessary foundation for the broader interpretation, which could never arise without them. Circle one is justly central, and circle two is an indispensable enlargement of its meaning. If God is real, he must be consciously knowable by human beings. If he is to make any real difference in human existence, he cannot be so far removed that encounter with him is impossible. Apart from some personal awareness of him in men's emotional, intellectual, and volitional experience, and apart from recognition of his involvement in the day-by-day lives of men and women, the religious dimension of human life would be greatly impoverished, if indeed it could ever have emerged. In the long run religious faith could mean little without a fairly widespread consciousness of men's relation to the ultimate ground of their existence. It is therefore imperative to cultivate and deepen, wherever possible, the personal sense of the presence of God.

Nevertheless, the fact remains that for multitudes today God is hidden, absent, or unreal. For various reasons any experience of divine reality consciously recognized as such seems closed to them. The investigation of a broadened understanding of religious experience therefore becomes a matter of practical relevance as well as theoretical significance. If the approaches to circles one and two are obscured, possibly the exploration of circle three may disclose alternative areas of meaning which are not only immensely valuable in themselves, but may ultimately prepare the way for a more personal awareness of God and the rich enhancement of life which this could make possible.

3 CONSCIOUS AWARENESS OF GOD

The heart of the religious life in its fullness is the personal relationship of men and women of faith to God. That relationship includes beliefs, but these are directed toward one who is encountered rather than merely believed in on hearsay or as the result of a convincing argument. The relation involves ethical action, but this occurs in trustful, dedicated response to the prior action of God. It concerns the whole of human existence, but existence seen always as dependent on its Ground. It embraces persons-in-community rather than isolated individuals, but the members are constituted a community primarily by their relation to a common center. As Martin Buber observes, "the circle is described by the radii, not by the points along its circumference." [1] In Judeo-Christian faith the center on which the radii converge is the ever-renewed personal experience of God and the living awareness of his presence. This awareness takes a variety of forms. It may involve, for example, a sense of finitude before the Infinite, of unworthiness in the presence of the Holy, of creatureliness before the Creator, or of newness of life bestowed

[1] *Paths in Utopia,* tr. R. F. C. Hull (London: Routledge & Kegan Paul, 1949), p. 135.

by supreme Grace. But always it comes to a focus in the God who is the ultimate Source of all these experiences.

The Old Testament writings are above all the consequence of the firsthand experience of men of faith who found God disclosing himself in their own lives and the life of their nation. Confronting the Lord amid the events of his time, the prophet proclaimed the divine will for his people. The psalms are the expression in temple worship of living encounters of responsive souls with the God whom they met in the heights and depths of their existence as Creator, Judge, and Redeemer. The drama of Job reaches its climax when Job emerges from his sufferings with the inner assurance which enables him to declare:

> I had heard of thee by the hearing of the ear,
> but now my eye sees thee (42:5).

This personal awareness appears in a new form in the joyous testimony of the New Testament writers to the healing, transforming power of God in Jesus Christ. The apostles and those who received their message knew themselves to be delivered from bondage to the freedom of the sons and daughters of God, and they attributed this knowledge to the witness of the Spirit himself (Rom. 8:15-16). In their fellowship with one another they were sustained constantly by the grace, peace, and love of God (Gal. 4:4-7). Filled with the Spirit, they spoke the word of God with boldness, and spread the Good News throughout the Greco-Roman world (Acts 4:31; cf. 4:20; Rom. 5:1-5; Eph. 3:16-19).

This kind of personal relationship between God and man has been normative throughout much of Christian history. Repeatedly Christians have failed to realize it in practice, yet the communion of each believer with God has been held up fairly consistently as a possibility and hence as a goal to be sought. Convincing evidence of its realization is found not only in the great mystics, but in the lives of countless others in all centuries. Notable instances appear in such varied forms as the courage given to Martin Luther to risk his life in opposing papal power, the Inner Light in George Fox and other Quakers, John Wesley's "experimental knowledge of Christ," and Martin Luther King's consciousness of divine support in his heroic struggle for the dignity and freedom of black people. The same phenomenon is manifest in the life of Gandhi; when he fasted and prayed, writes Erik Erikson, "the masses and even the English held their breath." [2]

As already noted, such occurrences seem to be less widespread in the late twentieth century than formerly. The sense of God's hiddenness is perhaps more frequently reported than the vivid consciousness of his presence. Nevertheless, many persons still testify to experiences in which they find God "closer than breathing, nearer than hands or feet." Many have learned that if they take time for the practice of spiritual disciplines and consciously relate their daily pursuits to the divine purposes, they can and do become aware of the divine presence.

In this as in other respects we who are immersed in the values and practices of a technological, highly urbanized culture may learn much from people of simpler cultures. For example, L. Harold DeWolf writes of observing in Rhodesia, where he lived for two extended periods, "the immediate sense of personal reality; the profound, direct impact of life and death; and the awesome awareness of God's presence so characteristic of African Christianity." He also noted among Rhodesian Christians an "all-consuming wholeness of faith." This impression closely parallels that made on my wife and me during a year of teaching (1969-70) at Union Theological Seminary near Manila, Philippines. We found among students and other Christians a depth of

---

[2] *Young Man Luther* (New York: W. W. Norton and Co., [1958] 1962), p. 262.

faith and commitment which contrasts sharply with the conventional religion often characteristic of church people in Western lands.

Yet even amid the superficiality and materialism of the West are widespread and varied evidences of sensitivity to a deeper dimension in religion. Although corporate worship in many churches continues to be traditional, drab, and unimaginative, experimentation with new forms of celebration in the community of faith manifests a vitality which participants gratefully ascribe to the action of God himself. Cases in point are such phenomena as folk masses and other services of worship, often led by young laymen, using contemporary words and music; the house churches and related small groups meeting regularly for Bible study, prayer, and social action; and the growth of the "Jesus people," for many of whom the bad trip of drug addiction has been replaced by a healthy-minded, outgoing journey in the company of one who renews and transforms life. When I met for a day in the fall of 1971 with about sixty United Methodist ministers of central Pennsylvania, I was frankly surprised to find that the majority of them reported among their young people a greater interest in the church than was the case a decade earlier, and this development was related in part to a sense of reality in the personal faith of the youth. In a seminar on the doctrine of the Holy Spirit held at Wesley Theological Seminary, Washington, D.C., during the first semester of 1971-72, each of the students enrolled testified in unassuming sincerity to one or more personal experiences which he or she interpreted as the work of the Holy Spirit.

Looking back on 1972, Religious News Service noted evidences of a new search for inner experience and meaning among the American people, and judged this to be the top religious development of the year. Explo '72 attracted 100,000 young people to the Cotton Bowl in Dallas for a training conference on evangelism.

The charismatic movement has registered noteworthy advances, chiefly among long-established religious bodies. In August, 1972, the first international Lutheran Conference on the Holy Spirit drew 8,000 to Minneapolis; and in June, 1973, 20,000 attended the seventh annual meeting of the Catholic Charismatic Renewal Movement at the University of Notre Dame. From 5,000 to 6,000 persons take part in weekly prayer meetings in the Boston Roman Catholic archdiocese. Each year since 1970 the Greater Pittsburgh Charismatic Renewal Movement has had to seek larger accommodations for its annual meetings.

Developments like these are of uneven worth, and they must be examined critically rather than taken at their face value. The movement which seeks to realize the gifts of the Holy Spirit may prove to be one of the most important events within ecumenical Christianity in this century. In its international, national, and regional manifestations it has become a source of new spiritual vitality and depth for many people. Yet so far it has not reached most church members at the congregational level. It has sometimes been weakened by concentration on individual salvation at the expense of social responsibility, by a tendency to make glossolalia normative for all Christians, and by other forms of theological rigidity. It is always in order to "try the spirits," to discern whether they are of God or represent merely subjective emotions or transitory fads. Yet such phenomena bear witness unmistakably to a seriousness of religious concern and a genuine conviction on the part of those involved that they are related positively to the life of God himself.

The nature of the experiences which give rise to this conviction can be much better understood if we move from broad characterization and summarization to concrete instances. There are for the mid-twentieth century no collections of empirical data comparable to those gathered by Starbuck and James three quarters of a century ago.[3] Nevertheless, from contemporary oral and printed sources many reliable accounts of personal religious experiences are available. From these several firsthand reports may be taken as representative.

Susumu Akahoshi, chief psychiatrist at Ogawa Red Cross Hospital, Tokyo, tells of his "conversion" at the age of eighteen. Engulfed in the anxieties and tensions of youth, he sought faith through reading the Bible and theological and philosophical writings, meditating, and praying. Reading Luther's *Preface to St. Paul's Epistle to the Romans,* he felt his "heart burn with faith," and was reminded of John Wesley's similar experience. Then one day during a walk on a low mountain path near his home he had "a mystical experience of unity with God as the absolute Being." "I felt," he writes, "the smallness, worthlessness, and sinfulness of myself, and at the same time I experienced great peace and the joy of being embraced in the bosom of the infinite and eternal God." Shortly thereafter Akahoshi wrote an article for a youth magazine in which he confessed his new-found faith and summarized his resultant religious thought. This brought such tranquillity that he recovered from stomach hyperchlorhydria from which he had suffered for years. These experiences have provided the basis for his later religious life, which has been marked not only by personal wholeness but by profound concern for the healing of other persons. For eighteen years he sought "to evangelize and care for the sick" as a chest surgeon in tuberculosis sanatoriums. More recently he has pursued similar goals through clinical work in psychotherapy, sustained continually by an awareness of the creative and renewing activity of God.[4]

[3] Edwin D. Starbuck, *The Psychology of Religion,* 3rd ed. (New York: Charles Scribner's Sons, 1911); William James, *The Varieties of Religious Experience.*

[4] Paul E. Johnson (ed.), *Healer of the Mind* (Nashville: Abingdon Press, 1972), pp. 39-41. This volume is a valuable collection of religious autobiographies by psychiatrists of four nationalities.

Paul Tournier, author of many books who has practiced medicine in Geneva since 1928, recounts an experience which came to his wife on a New Year's Eve. When he returned home from spending the moment of midnight in the cathedral square, he found her "overwhelmed and transformed." "I have suddenly realized for the first time the greatness of God!" she told him. "As the bells rang out, telling of the inexorable and endless march of time," it had come to her that God was infinitely greater than she had ever imagined. "God had spoken to her through the voice of the bells, and she had answered. . . . The greatest event in life had taken place: the personal encounter of Creator and creature, the dialogue between the voice of God . . . and the voice of man." The experience proved to be infectious, touching husband as well as wife. During the year that followed, writes Tournier, God "led us from experience to experience, to a renewing of our whole personal and professional life, calling us from ecclesiastical activity to a spiritual ministry." [5]

A somewhat similar experience under quite different circumstances is described by James A. Knight, Associate Dean and Professor of Psychiatry at the Tulane University School of Medicine, New Orleans. It occurred in the delivery room at Duke University Hospital during his internship, just after he had delivered a baby. As he waited for the completion of the physiological processes, he saw and heard the trickle of blood from the uterus indicating the separation of the placenta from the uterus. Soon the placenta was expelled and the uterus contracted, stopping the flow of blood. Knight continues:

While marveling at the mystery and miracle of each step in the birth process, I looked out of the window and saw the rays of the early morning sun illuminating the tower of the Duke University

---

[5] "A Religious Experience," *Problems and Perspectives in the Philosophy of Religion,* ed. George I. Mavrodes and Stuart C. Hackett (Boston: Allyn & Bacon, 1967), pp. 165-66.

Chapel. A most profound sense of the awareness and presence of the Holy overwhelmed me. My mind's ear seemed to hear a voice: "Put off your shoes from your feet, for the place on which you are standing is holy ground."

Knight testifies that this sense of religious awe has remained throughout his medical career. With the psalmist he declares: "I am fearfully and wonderfully made: marvelous are thy works" (Ps. 139:14 KJ). In particular he sees the body as the temple of God. "The awareness of His Presence in our very being makes for a spiritual sensitivity and acceptance that we belong to God." [6]

It is worthy of note that each of these accounts records the continuation in later life of the awareness and the attitude which characterized the particular event described. The same is true of several experiences of my own, two of which may be described here.

In the summer of 1949 I had a brief teaching engagement at Lake Junaluska, North Carolina. My family had accompanied me so that we could later enjoy some hiking and camping in the Great Smokies. On our return northward we spent one clear night under the stars, without erecting our tent, and were on our way early the next morning on the Blue Ridge Parkway in southern Virginia. The road wound alternately through majestic forests and beside pastures of the few remaining farms, with occasional views of deep valleys bathed in morning mist. So impressed were we by the beauty around us that we stopped at about 6:30 to have our family devotions by the roadside. Together we stood for a time without speaking, enthralled by the tinkling of the bells on the cattle in the nearby meadow, the glistening of the dew in the morning sun, and the peacefulness of the landscape surrounding us. Then we read together several stanzas of Harriet Beecher Stowe's hymn which begins:

[6] Paul E. Johnson (ed.), *Healer of the Mind,* p. 130.

Still, still with thee, when purple morning breaketh,
    When the bird waketh, and the shadows flee;
Fairer than morning, lovelier than daylight,
    Dawns the sweet consciousness, I am with thee.

Unlike the poet we were not alone. Yet wife and husband and a girl and a boy in their teens, united by family love, knew "the solemn hush of nature newly born" and felt the presence of him who sustains both nature and human life. The experience set the tone for the day that followed, and it has remained vividly etched in my memory ever since. Years later, when our son was applying for ordination and admission to membership in a Methodist Annual Conference, he cited this event as one of the influences which had led him toward the professional ministry as his lifework.

I am of course well aware of the harshness and violence as well as the beauty of the physical world, and of the suffering no less than the joy of our human lot. The negative factors must be faced unflinchingly in any religious interpretation of existence. However, some of the most persuasive reports of encounters with God concern events in which pain and awareness of finitude and mortality have played a central part. This has sometimes been true in my own experience.

One evening in December, 1955, a few days before Christmas, I lay in Massachusetts General Hospital recovering from a major operation, my second in six months. The night before, talented singers from the Harvard-Radcliffe Choral Society had gone through the halls cheering the patients with their moving carols. This evening there were no visible singers. But as I lay there alone in my discomfort I began reading the fortieth chapter of Isaiah. Suddenly I was no longer alone, but surrounded by angelic voices. Outside the temperature had dropped to zero, and the heating system was working overtime. In my radiator the steam throbbed rhythmically, while across the hall, as I later learned, water boiled noisily in the sterilizer. Yet what I heard was nothing so prosaic as steam or water, but celestial music.

Christmas carols filled the air—or rather a composition which was no one carol but all carols. In sublime harmonies akin to a Bach chorale the voices were singing the words I was reading: "Do you say, 'My way is hid from the Lord?' . . . Have you not heard? . . . The Lord is the everlasting God, the Creator of the ends of the earth. He does not faint or grow weary. . . . He gives power to the faint, and to him who has no might he increases strength. . . . They who wait for the Lord shall renew their strength."

I was lifted as on eagle wings into the very presence of God. I knew that in his power and love I would be ready for whatever might be in store for me, whether joy or pain, whether running in some noteworthy service or walking in routine tasks. The assurance has remained, even though a year later further surgery was necessary. Because of the nature of this event, its connection with the rest of my life, and its fruits, I cannot regard it as merely subjective. Reinforced by comparable experiences in later years, it constitutes for me one authentic manifestation of the reality of God.

Uppermost in the personal experiences just cited is the awareness of God as ultimate source of support, strength, and faith in the lives of human beings. However, this is only part of the picture, as was suggested already at the beginning of this chapter where man's sense of finitude and unworthiness was included among various forms of the divine-human encounter. In particular, it is important to point out the prominence in religious experience of the human consciousness of opposition and disobedience to God, guilt, and divine judgment. Appropriately, van der Leeuw's definitive work *Religion in Essence and Manifestation* includes chapters on both "The Avoidance of God" and "Enmity to God."

Paul Tillich makes clear that the term *God* is unsoundly used if it designates only a deity with which men can live comfortably, without tension.

A man who has never tried to flee God has never experienced the God Who is really God. . . . For there is no reason to flee a god who is the perfect picture of everything that is good in man, . . . who is simply the universe, or the laws of nature, or the course of history, . . . who is nothing more than a benevolent father, a father who guarantees our immortality and final happiness. Why try to escape from someone who serves us so well? No, those are not pictures of God, but rather of man, trying to make God in his own image and for his own comfort.[7]

It would be more accurate, therefore, to construe even the protest against and the rejection of God as themselves aspects of men's confrontation with the real God, who makes demands on us, including the commitment of our lives to him rather than our own limited ends. Hence any sound understanding of authentic experience of God must make wide room for man's uneasy conscience and his sense of sin in the presence of the God whom he has failed. The God of enlightened religious experience is a God of righteousness and justice; the more we find in him the transcendent yet immanent source of our highest values, the more we encounter him as Accuser and Judge when in self-will we break the relationship with him for which we were created.

Beginning with Adam and Eve, who sought to hide from God because they knew their disobedience and feared its consequences, the biblical writings offer abundant instances of human awareness of the divine disfavor. The first response of Isaiah to his vision of God in the temple is the cry: "Woe is me! For I am lost; for I am a man of unclean lips, and I dwell in the midst of a people of unclean lips; for my eyes have seen the King" (Isa. 6:5). Experiences akin to this are no doubt reflected in "the word of the

---

[7] *The Shaking of the Foundations* (New York: Charles Scribner's Sons, 1948), p. 42.

Lord" proclaimed by other prophets as well as Isaiah—a word which is often one of doom. Similarly, a recurrent theme of the Psalms is penitence; consciousness of sin produces "a broken and contrite heart."

The awareness of failure to fulfill God's righteous will is likewise integral to mature religious experience today. We have previously noted Susumu Akahoshi's conviction of his own "smallness, worthlessness, and sinfulness" in the presence of the same divine reality which gave him a sense of forgiveness and deliverance. Deep personal awareness of shared guilt appears also in the religious experience of David Calder Moir, Medical Officer at University College of Wales, Aberystwyth. Moir tells of working, during his final year as a medical student, in a Glasgow clinic for the treatment of venereal disease. Many of the patients were prostitutes. Though their disease was often arrested or cured, both they and those who treated them knew that they would return, since their lives seemed hopelessly enmeshed with those of their customers of the slums or the docks. Neither their lives nor their deaths would have any of the hope, the dignity, or the values which might make health possible or worth attaining. Confronting this reality, Moir's conception of his role as a doctor underwent radical change. He could no longer regard himself as a human benefactor dispensing medical benefits to those who needed them. Instead, he writes,

I was a member of the society that made such sickness and suffering possible, and that did not care. The guilt of these girls was my guilt too. Our common situation was one which called not for a doctor but for a redeemer. This, I suddenly realized, was what the gospel of Jesus Christ was all about.

This proved to be for the young physician "one of those moments in which truth is revealed." Though he feels that he has often been unfaithful to the truth thus disclosed, he remains certain of it, and he carries on his work sustained by it. He does not mention the word of God, but when following his reference to the gospel he writes of "the faith that would give reconciliation and wholeness to these broken girls and to me," it is clear that he attributes to divine activity both the disclosure of his shared guilt and the promise of healing.[8]

Moir's changed understanding of his task calls attention to two basic dimensions of the personal experience of God which have been implicit throughout this chapter, but which now need to be highlighted. One is the awareness of God as Redeemer. The confrontation with him who accuses and judges us need not be final; it is superseded by the meeting with one who heals and renews, restoring us to right relations with himself. Biblical faith speaks repeatedly of the Lord who is gracious and merciful, who in steadfast love blots out our transgressions, and who comes to seek and to save that which was lost (Pss. 130:7; 145:8; Isa. 43:25; Luke 19:10). Though the language used often differs, the same assurance is present in much contemporary religious life. Akahoshi describes the peace and joy of being forgiven and accepted by God; Moir writes of reconciliation and wholeness; and in my own experience on several occasions the grateful recognition of physical healing has been one facet of a much broader awareness of the renewing, transforming power of God in all aspects of my life.

The other dimension of religious experience requiring further specific explication is the call to acceptance of responsibility. Moses is called from following his flocks to lead his people out of bondage. Jeremiah is commissioned "to pluck up and to break down, to destroy and to overthrow, to build and to plant" (Jer. 1:10). Israel as a people is summoned not only to enter into a covenant with the Lord, but to become "a light to the nations" (Jer. 10:23; 11:3-5; 31:31; Isa. 49:1, 6). The church in the New

[8] Paul E. Johnson (ed.), *Healer of the Mind,* pp. 147-48.

Testament is a congregation called to ministry (Eph. 4:11-12; I Peter 2:9), and those who have been made new are entrusted with the message of reconciliation (II Cor. 5:17-20). Even so, the personal and professional renewal which followed the Tourniers' New Year's encounter moved them to accept a deep-level ministry to their fellow men and women. Akahoshi's religious faith has become the basis for a lifelong concern for the healing of the physically and emotionally sick. Moir's moment of truth has been likewise expanded to years of service in which his own relation to God finds expression in his effort to help other people find wholeness of life. Such occurrences exemplify a major characteristic of twentieth-century religious experience: personal sensitivity to the presence of God involves a call to mission, the acceptance in his name of some kind of responsibility for the well-being of people in the world.

Moreover, such responsiveness to the needs of other human beings often serves to deepen the awareness of God which evokes it. This reciprocal relation may be so intimate that it is impossible to distinguish separate components in one I-Thou-We experience.

The close connection between personal faith in God and sensitivity to human values was vividly illustrated in a series of events initiated by the Ninth General Synod of the United Church of Christ held at St. Louis in June, 1973. One of the social problems considered by the 780 delegates and 300-odd visitors was the plight of the long-exploited grape and lettuce pickers of California. These workers, largely Mexican-American migrants, had found new hope for fair hiring practices, just wages, decent working conditions, and human dignity through the United Farm Workers Union led by Cesar Chavez, whose Catholic faith integrates prayer, fasting, union organization, and nonviolent social action. Their goals and activities were opposed by most of the growers and the powerful Teamsters Union, who wanted to preserve the status quo.

When information came of efforts to destroy the UFWU

through intimidation and beatings of workers by hired goons, and when Chavez asked for the help of religious leaders willing to demonstrate their moral support by their physical presence, the synod responded by sending 95 delegates to California to spend a day in the Coachella valley as observers and picketers. A major share of their plane fare was covered by a special offering of $7,000 given in a worship service held in the Roman Catholic cathedral in St. Louis. Neither those who went nor the synod as a whole were under any illusions as to the long-range effect of this brief action on the outcome of the struggle, but they deemed it important in a time of crisis to identify the church unmistakably with the cause of the workers.

Following their return each of the 95 "pilgrims" was asked to tell the synod in a sentence one major impression of his or her experience. Some told of witnessing beatings of strikers and their families and the damaging of their cars by burly ruffians. Others spoke of the climate of threats and abuse surrounding the pickers as they sought liberation from exploitation. The house of one worker's family had been burned the night before the visit. Some reports described the abject poverty of the largely illiterate victims of economic and racist oppression.[9] Cesar Chavez had sent to the synod as a gift four crates of red grapes picked by UFWU members on the farm of a Jewish owner who had signed a contract with the union. Following the testimonies the grapes were passed among the worshipers as they sang,

> Let us drink wine together
> By God's grace.

The crushing of the fruit in the eating became powerfully sacramental—both a reenactment of the Last Supper of Jesus with his

---

[9] For a factual report and a balanced interpretation of the struggle of the grape pickers, see "Duel in the Sun; Union Busting, Teamster Style," *The Progressive,* July, 1973 (Vol. 37, No. 7), pp. 17-20.

disciples and an expression of solidarity with people whose lives are being crushed by exploitation today. Numerous participants were moved to tears, and many spontaneously embraced one another. Hundreds experienced an overwhelming sense of the presence of the God who is exalted in justice.[10]

On the following Sunday worshipers in the West Parish Congregational Church at West Barnstable, Massachusetts, were enabled through the creative imagination of the pastor to share a somewhat similar experience. A visitor at the Ninth General Synod, the Rev. David Waite Yohn, brought back from St. Louis a bunch of the Coachella valley grapes. In a celebration of the Lord's Supper these replaced grape juice in some of the communion cups, so that representative persons scattered through the congregation communed by eating grapes that vividly symbolized the personal ordeal of those whose toil had produced them. With my wife and some cherished friends, I was privileged to take part in this service. For all in our group it brought a seldom-felt sense of concrete reality to Holy Communion; it bound us together across a continent in loving concern with fellow human beings in their suffering; and it gave us a powerful awareness of the presence of the divine Spirit in whom such human strivings find their deepest support and their fullest meaning.

[10] Reporting on the St. Louis Synod, Marjorie Hyer criticized the Coachella valley pilgrimage and the ensuing reports as emotional expressions rather than a realistic response to the issues. In reply, Cesar Chavez wrote, "We were not only grateful that they came, but we believe that their presence with us was one important reason why the Teamsters withdrew their hired 'goons' a week after the UCC people were on the picket line." John R. Moyer, of the UCC Board of Homeland Ministries, asserted, "The trip . . . helped to bring about three things: the lifting of the farm workers' morale, the broadening of church support for poor people who want to build their own union, and a decision by the Teamsters the following week to call off their tactics of violence." (*The Christian Century*, 90 [1973], 750, 926.)

4 INTIMATIONS OF TRANSCENDENCE

Conscious experience of God of the kind just examined is apparently unknown to large numbers of people, including many who profess belief in God's reality. Nevertheless, there is considerable evidence that all human beings are conscious to some degree, however faintly, of a reality which transcends their own existence. For example, all men seem to have a primordial experience of being. This includes at least a vague immediate awareness not only of their own being, but also of being beyond their own, and perhaps even beyond that of the physical order. Although what is here often dimly perceived is not universally recognized as God, such an interpretation may well provide the most intelligible account of it. The same may be true of many other human experiences. Our common life contains a rich variety of intimations of a more-than-human reality which are often not understood as divine by the persons most directly concerned, but which may actually involve the living presence of God, acting as it were incognito.

The biblical writings themselves report numerous experiences of this nature. In the narrative in Genesis 18–19 the Lord appears to Abraham at Mamre when he provides hospitality for three wayfarers. Only after much conversation does Abraham become aware that one of his visitors is the Lord, who tells him that his wife Sarah will bear a son, and announces the impending destruction of Sodom and Gomorrah. Then the other two men, now referred to as angels, go on to Sodom, where they are given food and overnight lodging by Lot, who does not realize until the next day that they are messengers of the Lord. The possibility of an extension of this experience is suggested by the injunction of the author of the book of Hebrews: "Do not neglect to show hospitality to strangers, for thereby some have entertained angels unawares" (13:2). Genesis also records the story of Jacob on his journey from Beersheba toward Haran. He stops to spend the night in what appears to be an ordinary place, using a stone for a pillow. In a dream, however, he sees the Lord above a ladder connecting earth and heaven, and receives a far-reaching assurance of divine favor toward him and his descendants. When he awakes all is different: "Surely the Lord is in this place; and I did not know it. . . . How awesome is this place! This is none other than the house of God, and this is the gate of heaven" (28:10-22).[1]

The passage in Matthew (25:31-46) depicting the Last Judgment as a separation between the sheep and the goats is usually taken primarily as an admonition to the disciples of Jesus to minister to the needy as a service to God. Only those who demonstrate real concern for their fellows by concrete action to relieve suffering can expect to be welcomed into the Kingdom. But inseparably related to this meaning is another. Those who gave food, drink, clothing, and shelter to others who lacked such necessities and those who visited the sick and the prisoners were unconscious of the presence of God and unaware that they were doing his work: "Lord, when was it that we saw you hungry and

[1] Cf. the accounts of the appearances of God to Moses in the burning bush (Exod. 3:1-6) and to Elijah in "a still small voice" (I Kings 19:1-12).

fed you, or thirsty and gave you drink, a stranger and took you home, or naked and clothed you?" The king answers: "Anything you did for one of my brothers here, however humble, you did for me" (NEB). God is really present in our fellow men and women, and he is active in our deeds of loving concern, but he is often there incognito.

Luke's story of the journey to Emmaus provides another striking instance of the unrecognized presence of spiritual reality in events as commonplace as a walk and a meal. Filled with gloom following the crucifixion, two disciples were discussing their wrecked hopes. Although in the midst of their conversation Jesus himself joined them and walked along with them, "something kept them from seeing who it was." Even when their mysterious companion accepted their invitation to stay with them at evening they remained unaware of his identity. Finally, when at the table he broke and blessed the bread and offered it to them, "their eyes were opened, and they recognized him." Only then did they understand why they had felt their hearts to be "on fire" as he talked with them on the way (Luke 24: 13-35 NEB).

In view of the frequency of such accounts in the Hebrew-Christian Scriptures, it should occasion no surprise when secular literature and life are found to exhibit similar phenomena, with one important difference. Veiled awareness of the transcendent today, though fairly widespread, is less frequently accompanied by clear disclosure of the divine than in the biblical instances cited. Like the Athenians encountered by the apostle Paul, many people in our time have erected altars "to an unknown God" (Acts 17: 23). These altars are attitudes, responses, queries, and commitments which implicitly recognize a transcendent dimension but do not identify it as the activity of God.

The prevalence and the power of such experiences are attested by the works of a considerable number of contemporary interpreters who are not professional theologians or religionists, but

artists, poets, novelists, psychologists, social scientists, and others
who simply as thoughtful human beings seek to interpret various
aspects of the human situation. Theologians today have much to
learn from the reflections of these nonprofessionals who share
sensitively in the life of our time and in diverse ways report what
they find and what they think it means. Twentieth-century theology
has made much of the paradox of the hidden and revealed God.
Yet it has until recently devoted relatively little attention to the
hints of the divine presence hidden in the events of ordinary
human life not directly associated with religious activities as traditionally understood. Fruitful results may follow if this territory is
explored. This will entail a concerted effort to do theology (in
Pannenberg's words) "from below," attempting to survey the
human scene as such through the eyes of competent observers
who are seeking truth without primary regard for its religious
significance. This does not involve an attempt to ignore revelation
or faith, but the effort to take in all seriousness the given reality
of human life itself. It does not mean surrendering the vertical
reference; it calls rather for recognizing that the vertical may
intersect with a wider range of our horizontal experiences than has
been generally supposed.

To a limited degree this chapter and the remainder of this book
are an experiment in doing theology "from below." The inquiry
does not pretend to begin neutrally with a purely scientific investigation of the nature of man, and then to attempt to draw
objective conclusions growing out of the data. However, it does
endeavor to explore various aspects of the mystery of human life
with the help of sensitive thinkers who have no theological axe
to grind. Those to be examined have been led by their own
experience and disciplined study to affirm a transcendent dimension in human existence. Their approaches differ considerably, as
do the terms they use, but they all deal with empirical realities

which point beyond themselves, and which are therefore open to interpretation in the broad sense as experiences of God.

"Peak Experiences": Abraham H. Maslow

We have noted above that the lives of people who are religious in the historic sense exhibit many instances of experiences of special enlightenment and power which are regarded as revelatory of transcendent reality. In the analyses of the psychologist Abraham H. Maslow this reference beyond is likewise present in a wide variety of other occurrences which he calls "peak experiences." Maslow differentiates broadly between persons who are bent mainly on the gratification of needs or deficiencies and the self-actualizers who are motivated chiefly by desire for growth. These characteristics may apply to the same individual at different times, and ideally the former passes into the latter as the child grows to maturity. But empirically some people are mostly satisfiers of needs while others in confident self-actualization have reached a relatively "high level of maturation, health, and self-fulfillment."

Though peak experiences come more frequently to persons who are highly growth-motivated, they are also enjoyed on occasion by more average people. Such experiences are felt as self-validating, self-forgetful, ego-transcending moments which are intrinsically valuable. They may occur in love and friendship, aesthetic enjoyment, mystical awareness, flashes of insight reached through psychotherapy, artistic creation, the discovery of truth, or even the sense of physical achievement or well-being. The whole range of human value is fertile ground for peak experiences.

These experiences are closely related to what Maslow calls Being-cognition. "Episodes of self-actualization" contribute much to the knowledge of reality which comes to those who have them. Maslow does not identify the two; though peak experiences always feel like Being-cognition, some of them prove to be erroneous, providing an emotional lift without sound foundation. Nevertheless, many do bring true knowledge of Being. Self-actualizing persons are extraordinarily capable of "cognition of the essence, or 'is-ness,' or intrinsic structure and dynamics, and presently existing potentialities" of themselves and their world. Moreover, through their greater sensitivity and perceptiveness, the rest of us may gain a better understanding of reality than we could through our own eyes alone.

Authentic peak experiences thus point beyond themselves and beyond the persons who have them. We cannot command them; they simply happen to us. When they occur we respond "as before something great"—in wonder, awe, reverence, humility, and surrender. Seen as a whole, they seem to involve a dynamic parallelism between the inner and the outer. As the individual finds himself perceiving something of the essential Being of the world, he concurrently comes closer to the core of his own Being; he becomes more truly himself, more integrated, more fully human. Conversely, his "greatest attainment of identity, autonomy, or selfhood is itself simultaneously a transcending of itself, a going beyond and above selfhood." [2]

"The Unconscious God": Viktor Frankl

Though Maslow finds that men's experiences of intrinsic value provide intimations of Being deeper than or beyond the human, he does not use the term God to characterize this reality. In contrast, the Austrian psychiatrist Viktor Frankl is led by his

[2] *Toward a Psychology of Being*, 2nd ed. (New York: Van Nostrand Reinhold Co., [1962] 1968), pp. 27, 71, 79, 87-88, 95, 97-100, 105. For an illuminating study of "intensity experiences" which strongly resembles Maslow's analysis, see Marghanita Laski, *Ecstasy; a Study of Some Secular and Religious Experiences* (Bloomington: Indiana University Press, 1962).

researches in existential analysis and logotherapy to affirm that all men are related to God, though often they remain unconscious of his presence.

A major source of Frankl's interpretation is his investigation of questions having to do with meaning and value in human existence, triggered by his long imprisonment in Nazi concentration camps during World War II, when he did not know from day to day whether he would survive or suffer the death which did overtake his parents, his wife, and all other members of his family except one sister. Human values, he maintains, are of three main kinds: (1) creative—those achieved in creative action; (2) experiential—those realized in experiences of receptivity toward the world, exemplified by surrender to the beauty in nature or art; and (3) attitudinal, depending on one's attitude toward the limiting factors in his life. Even an existence which is apparently impoverished with respect to both creation and experience may still afford opportunity for realization of the third category of values. Though a person may be confronted by an unalterable destiny which he can only accept, he may still determine the attitude he will take toward it. The way in which a man accepts the plight he cannot avoid, "the way in which he bears his cross, what courage he manifests in suffering, what dignity he displays in doom and disaster, is the measure of his human fulfillment."

Since values of this kind can always be attained to some degree, human existence can never be completely meaningless. Rather, a man's life retains its meaning up to its last breath. As long as he is conscious he has responsibility for realizing the attitudinal values, and by his attitude he has an opportunity to influence the lives of others. To be human means to be conscious and to be responsible.[3]

[3] *The Doctor and the Soul; An Introduction to Logotherapy,* tr. Richard and Clara Winston (New York: Alfred A. Knopf, 1960), pp. 50-51,

Phenomenologically, therefore, the ultimate foundation of human being is consciousness and responsibility. These are synthesized in men's consciousness of having responsibility or being responsible. However, the deeper analysis of human existence carried out by the logotherapist—who seeks to heal through heightening the awareness of meaning—roots this consciousness of responsibility in an "unconscious spirituality" which ultimately involves a relation of the human I to a transcendent Thou. The unconscious *logos* in each person includes a spiritual dimension; to the instinctively unconscious *it* is added the spiritually unconscious *I*. This unconscious spirituality of the human ego discloses an unconscious depth from which come the great existentially genuine decisions.

Within this spirituality Frankl finds what he calls an unconscious religiosity or relatedness to God. This is a relation to the transcendent which is to man apparently an immanent relation, yet one which often remains latent. Just as with the disclosure of unconscious spirituality the *I* comes into view behind the *it,* so with the disclosure of unconscious religiosity the transcendent *Thou* is revealed behind the immanent *I*. The spiritually unconscious is thus disclosed as also a transcendent reality. Implicit in it is an unrecognized faith, which signifies that God is really intended by men although they remain unaware of the fact: by their very nature they have a relation to God which, though it is often unperceived, is nonetheless intentional. This God Frankl calls "the unconscious God."

This formulation does not mean that God is unconscious "in himself, for himself, and of himself." It means rather that he is not present *to our consciousness*—that we may be unaware of our relation to him because to us it is repressed and hidden.

---

122. Cf. Frankl, *Man's Search for Meaning* (New York: Washington Square Press, 1963).

Thus "the unconscious God" connotes "the hidden relation of man to the God who from man's side is hidden." [4] Nevertheless, even though obscured, God is real in the depths of the life of man. A perceptive analysis of concrete human existence, motivated by the search for a sound psychotherapy, discloses his presence as the transcendent ground of men's awareness of responsibility, their search for meaning, and their realization of values.

The Reality of the Interior Life: Robert N. Bellah

Complementing the psychological explorations so far considered are several investigations recently undertaken by sociologists. Particularly noteworthy are the proposals of Robert N. Bellah and Peter L. Berger. Bellah rejects the univocal interpretation of reality which he sees as characteristic of our pseudoscientific culture. This view falsely assumes that science alone relates us to the objectively real. Actually, in the inner life of men we find such an overwhelming reality that it cannot be dismissed as simply "subjective." It exhibits a "constraining" quality, an "objectivity" which must enter into any judgments we make about the truth of our total human experience. The same is true of the group relations of men. We do not stand outside or over against reality; rather we actively participate in it. When we recognize this, we discover in our ordinary life itself vehicles for transcendence which enable us to make symbolic statements about reality and to bring coherence to the whole of our experience. Bellah lists three such dimensions.

(1) The "externality" of the inner life is definitely disclosed in the unsatisfied longings so characteristic of much of our human existence—the "deficiency needs" identified by Maslow. Such unsatisfied needs eloquently attest the need for change in the existing

[4] *Der unbewusste Gott* (Wien: Amandus-Verlag, 1949), pp. 89-93, 103.

situation, and hence convey truth about the structure of reality. (2) Transcendent reality is indicated likewise by the opposite kind of experience, that of fulfillment, illustrated in historic religion by feelings of healing, wholeness, and well-being, but found also more broadly in realizations of aesthetic, social, ethical, and recreational value. (3) There is also a kind of "collective interior" in human life. In religion as in other areas individual experience must be checked with the experience of other persons; individual growth requires group support and a network of interpersonal relations. Thus in society also we encounter something that is structural in reality. Especially noteworthy is the fact that society makes us aware of history, the contingencies and catastrophes of which are a proving ground for our personal and social values. Before the judgment of history we learn the inadequacy of every empirical society. "Every society is itself forced to appeal to some higher jurisdiction, to justify itself not entirely on its actual performance but through its commitment to unrealized goals or values." No society can avoid the resort to some symbolism to express its value commitments and support their legitimacy. The resulting symbols, such as God, Being, Nothingness, and Life, do not stand for any scientifically verifiable realities, but neither are they merely subjective. They intend to overcome all subject-object dichotomies and relate the manifold elements of our lives in a coherent whole. In individual and social experience we encounter a more-than-ordinary reality which impinges on ordinary reality, lays bare its pretensions, and imparts to it meaning and wholeness.[5]

Religious experience and symbolization are thus seen as structural in human life; religion is as central as speech to the self-definition of man. However, Bellah's "symbolic realism" is un-

[5] *Beyond Belief; Essays on Religion in a Post-Traditional World* (New York: Harper & Row, 1970), pp. 198-202, 245.

concerned about the cognitive claims of religious belief. He vigorously opposes the "objective cognitive bias" which holds that valid knowledge must always take the form of falsifiable scientific hypotheses. Reality is richly diversified; to deal adequately with it men must often use "nonobjective symbols that express the feelings, values, and hopes of subjects, or that organize and regulate the flow of interaction between subjects and objects, or that attempt to sum up the whole subject-object complex or even point to the context or ground of that whole." [6] Such symbols cannot be reduced to empirical propositions. They are noncognitive and nonscientific, but they are constitutive of persons and society. They are, moreover, much better fitted for dealing with the reality with which religion is concerned than the attitude which construes religious faith primarily in cognitive terms.

Religion is "a reality *sui generis*. To put it bluntly, religion is true," since it is intrinsic in the structure of human existence. As actually lived, therefore, religious faith is beyond both belief and unbelief; questions of cognitive truth and validity are largely irrelevant. The really important thing is that religious symbols, when personally appropriated, enable us to experience meaning in our existence and to bring to a focus what that meaning is.[7]

"Signals of Transcendence": Peter L. Berger

Peter L. Berger is as concerned as Bellah to assert the multiform nature of the reality encountered in human life, the depth and range of our experience of values, and the falsity of any attempt to compress all the data into the ways of knowing appropriate to the natural sciences. However, he differs markedly from Bellah in recognizing both cognitive significance and objectivity in our apprehension of transcendent reality. His views are clearly stated

---

[6] *Ibid.,* pp. 251-52.
[7] *Ibid.,* pp. 223, 240-41, 253, 204-5.

in *A Rumor of Angels; Modern Society and the Rediscovery of the Supernatural.*[8] As a social scientist Berger begins with the experiences of everyday human life—data which do not depend on an alleged divine revelation but which are available to all observers. Here we are likely to encounter a large array of human projections, which are taken by thinkers like Feuerbach and Freud to undermine the truth claims of religious faith. In Berger's view, however, if we turn from the projections to the projector and scrutinize the empirical data, we discover beneath the projections indications of "a reality that is truly 'other' and that the religious imagination of man ultimately reflects." [9]

In the human situation as given are phenomena which, though they are within the realm of "natural" reality, seem to point beyond it. These are "prototypical human gestures," "certain reiterated acts and experiences" which appear to express man's essential being. They are not "unconscious," needing to be excavated from the depths of the personality; rather they are a part of our ordinary awareness. They constitute for Berger "signals of transcendence" or "rumors of angels"—since angels traditionally are messengers of God. Though within the presuppositions of our naturalistic culture transcendence is only a rumor, the rumor may be traced to its source and discovered to be well grounded after all. Berger does not pretend to offer proof for his conclusions, and he recognizes that the transition from empirical to metaphysical reality is an act of faith. Yet for him the faith is eminently justified: belief in the transcendent offers a better account of the full range of human experience than the rigid, circumscribed naturalism which jauntily claims scientific validity.

The theological enterprise should consider all that can be empirically ascertained about men and their works, particularly the findings of the socio-historical sciences and philosophical

[8] (Garden City, N. Y.: Doubleday & Co., 1969).
[9] *Ibid.,* pp. 59, 90.

anthropology; the contents of all the religious traditions; and the data of men's aesthetic and ethical experience. The artistic "creations of Bach or Mozart, of Gothic cathedral builders, or of Chagall, Hölderlin, or Blake" are no less pertinent than the phenomena of physiology or biology.[10]

Among the human gestures which may be regarded as signals of transcendence Berger selects five for brief discussion:

1. Man's propensity for order. When a mother reassures an anxious child at night with the words, "Don't be afraid—everything is in order, everything is all right," she transcends the immediate situation to affirm her fundamental trust in reality as such. This exemplifies a broadly observable human tendency to order reality, in which "there is an intrinsic impulse to give cosmic scope to this order." Implied in such an extension is the belief not only that human order somehow reflects an order which transcends it, but that this transcendent order is worthy of men's ultimate trust.

2. The ability to interrupt time with play. As Johan Huizinga suggests, man is by nature *homo ludens*. Even when facing death and disaster men are capable of making jokes, writing poems, and carrying on metaphysical discussions. Children become so intent on their games that they grow oblivious to the outside world. Even the entry of the Soviet army into Vienna in 1945 interrupted the concert schedule of the Vienna Philharmonic Orchestra only about a week. Such events assert the ultimate supremacy of human gestures of beauty and creativity over actions of destruction. Experiences like joyful play, occurring in men's ordinary lives, manifest an inner intention which points beyond itself to a "supernatural" reality.

3. Orientation toward the future in hope. Human hope appears most intense when seemingly confronted by the threat of utter defeat, above all the final defeat of death. This is evidenced by

[10] *Ibid.*, pp. 65-66, 120-21, 106-7.

death-defying acts of courage motivated by hope for the attainment of justice or creative fulfillment. The capacity thus to say "No!" to death appears to be inherent in the being of man. The hope that makes such courage possible manifests itself in men's ordinary experience, but it implies intentions which outrun experience and transcend empirical reason in the expectation of ultimate vindication.

4. The conviction that acts of men which outrage justice are not merely despicable, but damnable. Such deeds as Eichmann's part in the Nazi massacres of the Jews call forth condemnation in absolute terms which reject as inadmissible all relativizing socio-historical explanations. Moreover, the intention of the condemnation extends beyond the confines of this world. Both the absoluteness and the cosmic reference signal transcendence. Some events in the war in Vietnam elicit similar responses. There are acts which call forth not only extreme censure, but *damnation* in the full religious sense of the term: their perpetrators not only exclude themselves from the normal human community; they also separate themselves finally from a moral order which transcends the community of men, thereby invoking a more-than-human retribution. The transcendence here suggested is the negative side of that expressed in the mother's reassurance of the frightened child by the affirmation that reality can be trusted.

5. Humor, which provides an ultimately religious vindication of joy. The fundamental element in the comic in human life is incommensurability or incongruity. At the heart of all other comic discrepancies is that between man and the universe. *"The comic reflects the imprisonment of the human spirit in the world"* (italics Berger's), but by laughing at it humor in effect declares that the captivity "is not final but will be overcome." This hint of redemption is another signal of transcendence. Basically the clown is not merely frivolous; by moving us to laugh at his predicament he is telling us that we can also laugh at our human plight and thereby surmount it through our relation to a greater reality.

In these and related ways, Berger believes, our everyday experience points beyond itself to the reality of the "God who is not the world and who was not made by man, . . . who is not a sign of human things but of whom human things are signs, who is symbolized and not a symbol." This is the God of the biblical tradition, who is affirmed equally by Christians, Jews, and Muslims, and who is the foundation of order, justice, and compassion in human life.[11]

"Pseudonyms of God": Ignazio Silone; Rainer Maria Rilke

Affirmations of transcendence among artists, poets, and novelists inevitably take a form quite different from the closely reasoned interpretations of behavioral scientists. However, in a considerable number of aesthetic and literary works may be found a message strikingly parallel to that voiced by the psychologists and sociologists already discussed. Indeed, in the arts that message is proclaimed with peculiar power. The authors of a perceptive interpretation of Rilke speak of a "mysterious philosophical undertow" in his elegies and sonnets which "creates that impression of something greater than art which great works of art produce." [12] We turn now to look at that something greater in a novel by the Italian Ignazio Silone and several short stories by Ranier Maria Rilke (1875-1926).

The action of Silone's *Bread and Wine* occurs in Italy in the mid-thirties of this century, during Mussolini's imperialistic invasion of Ethiopia. The central character, Pietro, is a leader in the underground struggle against the war and in behalf of a new order in Italian society. Even though Pietro, earlier a candidate

[11] *Ibid.*, pp. 65-94, 112.
[12] "Rilke, Rainer Maria," by Eliza Marian Butler and James Blair Leishman, *Encyclopaedia Britannica* (1971), Vol. 19, p. 335*b*.

for the priesthood, declares that he has lost his faith, the old priest Don Benedetto, his former teacher, finds God operating in Pietro's social activism:

> In times of conspiratorial and secret struggle, the Lord is obliged to hide Himself and assume pseudonyms. . . . Might not the ideal of social justice that animates the masses today be one of the pseudonyms the Lord is using to free Himself from the control of the churches and the banks?

Considering the major political expression of the demand for social justice in Italy in the 1930s, Silone is in effect asserting that the hand of God might be acting more truly among the Italian communists than among the priests and bankers who profess belief in him.

Elsewhere Don Benedetto returns to the same theme:

> This would not be the first time that the Eternal Father felt obligated to hide Himself and take a pseudonym. . . . He has never taken the . . . name men have fastened on Him very seriously; quite to the contrary, He has warned men not to name Him in vain as His first commandment. And then, the Scriptures are full of clandestine life. Have you ever considered the real meaning of the flight into Egypt? And later, when he was an adult, was not Jesus forced several times to hide himself and flee from the Judeans?

Thus God is seen as present in the struggle of Pietro and his comrades for justice, though he is in effect denied by the formal and socially indifferent worship of the church where his name is most loudly proclaimed. The fact that Pietro himself lives in disguise through most of the story is itself a suggestion that God does much of his work incognito.

A different intimation of the divine propensity to act in unexpected ways occurs during a conversation in Don Benedetto's home regarding God's coming to Elijah not in the earthquake, wind, or fire, but in a silence "like a rustling in the bushes, moved

by the evening breeze." As the friends talked a slight wind began
to stir in the garden, the trees rustled, and the door to the living
room creaked and opened. " 'What's happening?' said Martha
from the next room. Pietro shivered. The old man . . . said with
a laugh, 'Don't be afraid. You have nothing to be afraid of.' "
Then he "got up and closed the door which the evening breeze
had opened." Thus Silone moves from the Elijah story to a subtle
suggestion that God makes himself known in the personal intimacy
of close friends and their common commitment to freedom and
peace.[13]

Though Rilke's major contribution to world literature was made
through his poetic writings, he is of interest in the present context primarily because of a little—and little-known—book of short
stories entitled *Stories of the Dear God*.[14] A number of these
depict God as appearing on earth, unidentified, in ordinary persons and situations, especially in wayfarers from distant places.
For example, in "The Strange Man" a stranger arrives at the
storyteller's house at evening, where he is told of the time when
God sent his right hand to earth, commanding it to assume the
form of a man in order to bring him knowledge concerning his
finished creation, especially human beings. However, the hand
in human guise encountered much hostility which culminated on
a mountain where "men in iron clothing" inflicted on it such
suffering that "the whole earth was red from the blood of God,"
and no one could comprehend the horrible thing that had happened. With prodigious exertion God recalled his right hand, but
it had suffered so intensely that it has not yet recovered, and
continues to suffer in memory.

After a long pause the stranger asks, "Why have you told me
this story?" The storyteller replies, "Otherwise who would have

[13] *Bread and Wine* (New York: Athenaeum Publishers, [1946] 1962),
pp. 112, 247-48, 273-75, 294.
[14] *Geschichten vom lieben Gott* (Leipzig: Insel-Verlag, 1918).

understood me? You come to me without rank, office, or any kind of temporal status, almost without name. It was dark as you entered, only I noticed in your features a similarity—." When the stranger looks up questioningly, the host continues, "Yes, often I think perhaps God's hand is again on the way."

In "The Song of Righteousness" a blind old man, Ostap, appears in a group of soldiers one night and sings three sad songs bewailing the lack of righteousness in the world, then disappears into the night and goes on to sing his songs in the next village. A listener waits for more, then says with astonishment, "Now, why don't you stop? It's just as in the story of the betrayal. This old man was God." Whereupon another listener exclaims, trembling, "O, and I did not know it."

On occasion the divine presence is even less clearly discernible, but it is nonetheless real. "A Story Told to the Darkness" includes an incident having to do with seemingly unrewarded waiting for God. During a visit from Dr. Georg Lassmann, a childhood playmate, Frau Klara tells of an evening in her early life when the whole family awaited a very special guest, a wealthy relative from a distant place. They made many preparations and waited eagerly, but the guest did not come. Admitting her disappointment, Klara insists, "But it was still lovely." When Georg asks how this could be she replies, "In this way—the waiting, the many lamps, the quietness, the festive atmosphere." [15]

For both Silone and Rilke the arena of divine action is as broad as human life. Partly because of the finitude, the dim-sightedness, and the self-centeredness of men and partly because of the sheer mystery of the divine, God often works pseudonymously and is encountered in guises which leave in doubt his real identity. Yet sensitive persons find in ordinary experience persuasive hints that behind all outward appearances it is he who is the ultimate meaning of our existence.

[15] *Ibid.,* pp. 19-27, 69-88, 171-91.

"Times of Inherent Excellence": Wallace Stevens

In the poetry of Wallace Stevens (1879-1955) the element of transcendence is much more elusive and difficult to define than in either Rilke or Silone. Only rarely, and then indirectly, does he link it with God or the divine, and some of his allusions to God or the gods concern not their reality but the role of men in creating them. Yet no attentive reading of his poems can miss a dimension of depth which is closely akin to that found in the other thinkers so far examined.

The central concern of Stevens' poetry was to relate the claims of imagination and reality—a concern which in his later years led him to recognize the approximate equality and synthesis of the two worlds. Both are categorically affirmed. "The ultimate value," he writes, "is reality." Hence we look for nothing beyond it.[16] In the skeleton plan for a poem found in his papers after his death one of the opening lines reads, "I must impale myself on reality." [17]

Yet just as real as any external order is the poet's interior world, referred to in the title of one of Stevens' poems as "The Hermitage at the Center." The human imagination contributes something essential to the reality it finds. It is "description without place," "a sense to which we refer experience, a knowledge incognito." Such description

> is an expectation, a desire,
> A palm that rises up beyond the sea,
>
> A little different from reality:
> The difference that we make in what we see.

[16] *The Collected Poems of Wallace Stevens* (New York: Alfred A. Knopf, [1954] 1968), pp. 166, 471.

[17] *Opus Posthumous,* ed. Samuel French Morse (New York: Alfred A. Knopf, [1957] 1966), p. xxiv.

Thus there is no such thing as "a bare fact." In the passage where Stevens states that the ultimate value is reality he immediately adds, "Realism is a corruption of reality." There are in us "delicate clinkings not explained"; as a result, our experience is not flat but multi-dimensional.[18]

> . . . We seek
> Nothing beyond reality. Within it
>
> Everything, the spirit's alchemicana
> Included, the spirit that goes roundabout
> And through included, not merely the visible,
>
> The solid, but the movable, the moment,
> The coming on of feasts and the habits of saints,
> The patterns of the heavens and high, night air.[19]

Reality, therefore, is far richer and deeper than "the mere objectiveness of things" as portrayed by the "rigid realists." Bathed by the moonlight of the imagination, the landscape of our human existence "is active with a power, an inherent life." [20]

Stevens warns against sense empiricism as the way to truth:

> It is not in the premise that reality
> Is a solid. It may be a shade that traverses
> A dust, a force that traverses a shade.

With equal vigor he rejects the narrow rationalism which denigrates the emotional and intuitive aspects of human life. He applauds those theologians today who are articulating "a supreme need"—the need "to infuse into the ages of enlightenment an awareness of reality adequate to their achievements and such as will not be attenuated by them." [21]

---

[18] *Collected Poems*, pp. 505, 344, 340; *Opus Posthumous*, p. 166.
[19] *Collected Poems*, pp. 471-72.
[20] *Ibid.*, pp. 469-70, 531-32.
[21] *Ibid.*, p. 489; *Opus Posthumous*, p. 238.

Nevertheless, amid all this insistence on the rights of the imagination the poet is saved from uncontrolled subjectivism by his abiding respect for a reality which human beings find rather than create—"a reality which forces itself upon our consciousness and refuses to be managed and mastered." Poetry itself provides "contact with reality as it impinges on us from the outside, the sense that we can touch and feel a solid reality which does not wholly dissolve itself into the conceptions of our own minds." This function poetry can perform because it deals with reality in its concrete and individual forms, which cannot be discovered through the search for structure or pattern, "the apprehension of rational connections." The wonder and mystery of both art and religion is that they mediate "a reality not ourselves," revealing "something 'wholly other' by which the inexpressible loneliness of thinking is broken and enriched." [22]

Thus Stevens is concerned to maintain a delicate balance between things as they are and things as they are experienced by sensitive persons. This appears in delightful simplicity in "The Man with the Blue Guitar," which opens with these lines:

> The man bent over his guitar,
> A shearsman of sorts. The day was green.
>
> They said, "You have a blue guitar,
> You do not play things as they are."
>
> The man replied, "Things as they are
> Are changed upon the blue guitar."
>
> And they said then, "But play, you must,
> A tune beyond us, yet ourselves,
>
> A tune upon the blue guitar
> Of things exactly as they are."

[22] *Opus Posthumous*, pp. 235-38.

Yet an "exact" rendition of things as they are includes much more than appears on the surface. The guitarist later speaks of "the rhapsody of things as they are," and declares,

> Here I inhale profounder strength
> And as I am, I speak and move
>
> And things are as I think they are
> And say they are on the blue guitar.[23]

All the elements which are emphasized in Stevens' view of reality as experienced—its independent existence, its particularity, its manysidedness and depth, its dynamic, rhapsodic movement—are beautifully summed up when he writes:

> . . . Perhaps
> The truth depends on a walk around a lake,
>
> A composing as the body tires, a stop
> To see hepatica, a stop to watch
> A definition growing certain and
>
> A wait within that certainty, a rest
> In the swags of pine-trees bordering the lake.
> Perhaps there are times of inherent excellence,
>
> As when the cock crows on the left and all
> Is well, incalculable balances,
> At which a kind of Swiss perfection comes
>
> And a familiar music of the machine
> Sets up its Schwärmerei, not balances
> That we achieve but balances that happen.
>
> As a man and woman meet and love forthwith,
> Perhaps there are moments of awakening,
> Extreme, fortuitous, personal, in which

[23] *Collected Poems,* pp. 165, 183, 180.

> We more than awaken, sit on the edge of sleep,
> As on an elevation, and behold
> The academies like structures in a mist.[24]

Paradoxically, Stevens indicates that reality as he encounters it is also fictive: "The final belief is to believe in a fiction, which you know to be a fiction, there being nothing else. The exquisite truth is to know that it is a fiction and that you believe in it willingly." [25] However, it would be a mistake to conclude from this that Stevens is at heart a skeptic. By speaking of fiction he is simply calling attention to the inevitable characteristic of all our apprehensions of the real. All knowledge is a human construct; our minds contribute to the reality we know, and we can know it only in terms of the capacities which are ours. Thus Stevens can write, "We believe without belief, beyond belief." [26] Even our best interpretations of reality are provisional. Our symbolisms are always partial, subject to correction and modification.

Nevertheless, in "times of inherent excellence" we are awakened to realities beyond ourselves, a world unfathomed by those who search prosaically for supposedly objective facts—"a tidal undulation underneath." To the poet is disclosed life

> As it is, in the intricate evasions of as,
> In things seen and unseen, created from nothingness,
> The heavens, the hells, the worlds, the longed for lands.

In "The Final Soliloquy of the Interior Paramour," writing of our knowledge and the mystery of reality Stevens seems to voice his essential view in the words:

> We say God and the imagination are one . . .
> How high that highest candle lights the dark.

[24] *Ibid.*, p. 386.
[25] *Opus Posthumous*, p. 163.
[26] *Collected Poems*, p. 336.

Significantly, the last of the *Collected Poems* suggests that the candle discloses, however dimly, something that is really there. A bird's cry at dawn in early March, "a scrawny cry from outside," was

> A chorister whose c preceded the choir,
> It was part of the colossal sun,
>
> Surrounded by its choral rings,
> Still far away. It was like
> A new knowledge of reality.[27]

"The Transformations of God": Ernst Barlach

Similar intimations of a reality, elusive but genuine, transcending the visible are found in the creations of many artists who work with brush and chisel. John Dewey voices his conviction that we are citizens of a "vast world beyond ourselves" which is "the deeper reality of the world in which we live in our ordinary experiences." A work of art deepens and clarifies "that sense of an enveloping, undefined whole that accompanies every normal experience." It "elicits and accentuates this quality of being a whole and of belonging to the larger, all-inclusive whole which is the universe in which we live." [28] This quality is readily apparent in the work of painters like Vincent van Gogh and Marc Chagall. It is especially characteristic of the sculptures and drawings of the German Ernst Barlach (1870-1938).

Various passages in Barlach's letters and his diary call attention to the paradox of the presence of God in this world and the radical otherness of the world in relation to God; for him all events exhibit a kind of polar tension between the here and the beyond. He writes of profound inner stirrings which he can regard only as

---

[27] *Ibid.*, pp. 423, 486, 524, 534.
[28] *Art as Experience* (New York: G. P. Putnam's Sons, [1934] 1958), p. 195.

contacts with a "life-secret" at the core of his being. "On this rests my humanity; it is my root, from which springs for me the urge toward the highest." [29] Inevitably this finds expression in his artistic works, in which again and again the physically real reflects a deeper reality beyond it.

In Barlach's sketches and sculptures the gestures of glancing upward, listening attentively, kneeling, guarding with upraised arm, and being overwhelmed or deeply moved witness in changing visible forms to an invisible Thou by whom his characters feel confronted. Each moment is a fragment of eternity; each finite event, whether in nature or human life, mirrors the infinite. For example, in the drawing captioned "The Invisible" a man and woman seek to protect themselves against a storm, both the strength and interior nature of which are suggested by a falling chair, while the facial expressions portray not only fright but also a sturdy faith.

The same theme recurs in Barlach's woodcarvings "Wanderer in Wind" and "Shepherd in Storm," his charcoal sketch "Shepherd in Storm," and his ceramic statue "Woman in Wind." These works are a parable of life as the artist saw it: Human beings are confronted, and often buffeted, by an invisible and mysterious power which arouses their awe and fascination, and which calls on them to respond in trust, courage, and resolute purpose. Of such a relation the wind is a fitting symbol: to face it requires struggle, yet if it is strong enough it may be leaned on for support. "The wind blows where it wills, and you hear the sound of it, but you do not know whence it comes or whither it goes; so it is with every one who is born of the Spirit" (John 3:8).

Typical of the invisible for Barlach is the intermittent quality of its manifestation. God, he writes, "conceals himself behind everything, and in everything are narrow cracks through which he . . . shines and flashes, . . . cracks so fine that we can never

[29] Friedrich Dross (ed.), *Ernst Barlach: Leben und Werk in seinen Briefen* (München: Piper-Bücherei, 1952), pp. 86-87.

find them again if we only turn our heads." Only in rare moments of blessing, suddenly and unforgettable, the veil is lifted. That which is above and behind the visible comes momentarily into sight, then disappears again. Even Barlach's human figures seem often to stand in a twilight where nothing is neat or precise. They too arise out of the mystery of existence; nevertheless, they truly disclose aspects of that mystery.

Much of the essence of Barlach's intuition of reality is captured in the title of his collection of seven woodcuts which he calls *The Transformations of God* (*Die Wandlungen Gottes*). The phrase does not mean that God himself changes, but that his presence in the world takes shape in varied ways. That which ultimately moves men and women as the depth and ground of their being, and which makes particular claims on them, comes to expression at particular times in constantly changing forms. The transcendent God meets us here amid the flow of earthly life, with its ever-new situations, demands, crises, and opportunities.

Not only the woodcuts which bear the special title, but also a considerable number of the other works of Barlach might quite appropriately be designated together as "Transformations of God." Thus his "Love in Sorrow" depicts two men supporting a bereaved friend with their tender care. His "Good Samaritan" portrays the bowed form of the rescuer as he strains every muscle to lift the limp, half-dead victim out of the ditch. In "The Tired One" an angelic figure seeks in loving concern to restore the strength of a man exhausted by a long journey on foot. The beautiful wood carving "Rest on the Flight" pictures the babe cradled in the lap of his seated mother, who in turn is sheltered by the cloak which Joseph holds above her. The viewer is led almost unavoidably to reflect that above and around all three is a fourth presence, the guarding, sustaining power of the God whose holy purpose is embodied in this little family. In all these works, as in those depicting the impact of wind and storm, the artist seems to be saying that in and through a variety of ordinary human situations an extraordinary, more-than-human reality is creatively and redemptively at work in ever-changing ways. Appearing in different guises, he may pass unrecognized even by those most intimately involved, but he is nonetheless decisively active in the events portrayed.[30]

Summary

The survey of the psychological, sociological, literary, and artistic works of a variety of perceptive interpreters of human life sheds much valuable light on the nature of religious experience. When full allowance is made for the considerable diversity encountered, fundamental agreements appear which can be stated fairly accurately in a series of six propositions.

1. Our ordinary human existence exhibits an amazing richness, manysidedness, and depth, including many features which cannot be adequately described by the precise quantitative methods of the natural sciences.

2. Especially notable among these are experiences having to do with basic meanings and with personal and social values.

3. The empirical reality of such attitudes and events is not subject to question.

[30] Little has been published on Barlach in English. Of the German publications which contain selected reproductions of his artistic works, two are especially valuable: Carl D. Carls (ed.), *Ernst Barlach: Das plastische, graphische und dichterische Werk* (Berlin: Rembrandt Verlag, 1954); and Günter Gloede, *Barlach: Gestalt und Gleichnis* (Hamburg: Furche Verlag, 1966). For fuller coverage see the two volumes edited by Friedrich Schult: *Ernst Barlach: Das graphische Werk* and *Ernst Barlach: Das plastiche Werk,* published by Furche Verlag in Hamburg respectively in 1958 and 1960. A comprehensive bibliography may be found in Gloede's *Barlach,* pp. 153-59. For a helpful interpretation of *The Transformations of God (Die Wandlungen Gottes),* see Rudolf Bultmann, *Glauben und Verstehen,* IV (Tübingen: J. C. B. Mohr [Karl Siebeck], 1965), pp. 111-12, 126-27.

4. Sensitively apprehended, these experiences point beyond themselves to a transcendent dimension in the lives of human beings.

5. Such intimations of a reality deeper than either the natural or the human are frequently not perceived as divine by the persons most immediately involved.

6. Some interpreters are content to emphasize the importance of transcendent mystery without viewing it in theistic terms, while others ascribe the events experienced to the presence of God acting pseudonymously or incognito.

Our investigation thus tends strongly to support the tentative judgment expressed in Chapter Two that the experience of God should be conceived much more broadly than has traditionally been the case. The work of sensitive persons who are not professional theologians discloses an impressive body of data which must be taken seriously by all whose central concern includes the effort to understand the meaning and truth of the relation of men and women to God.

Indeed, theologians in increasing numbers are calling attention to such data. Thinkers like Charles Hartshorne, John E. Smith, and Sam Keen are stressing men's universal awareness of extra-human reality, especially their experience of value, which is unintelligible unless referred to transcendent reality or God. Huston Smith ventures "the possibility that reality includes surprising corridors of worth that elude ordinary eyes." [31] Langdon Gilkey dedicates two lengthy chapters to a discussion of "dimensions of ultimacy" in secular life, finding in each important aspect of our being—"our existence, our search for meaning, our knowing, our valuing, and our search for identity, community, and hope"— indications of an ultimate and unconditioned order which repre-

[31] Herbert W. Richardson and Donald W. Cutler (eds.), *Transcendence* (Boston: Beacon Press, 1969), p. 16.

sents the activity of God whether he is recognized or not.[32] Robert McAfee Brown, taking his cue from Ignazio Silone, has devoted his most recent book to a wide-ranging examination of *The Pseudonyms of God.*[33]

This whole area merits further exploration. The chapters that follow are an attempt to understand the theological implications of a number of features of our experience which seem to be ingredient to human existence as such, which often are not theistically interpreted, but which may deserve to be regarded as authentic manifestations of the divine presence.

---

[32] *Naming the Whirlwind: The Renewal of God-language* (Indianapolis: Bobbs-Merrill, 1969), p. 307; cf. pp. 305-413.

[33] (Philadelphia: The Westminster Press, 1972).

PART

2

INCOGNITOS OF GOD—FORMS OF HIS
UNRECOGNIZED PRESENCE

5 THE DEPTH IN EXISTENCE

A careful look at the intimations of transcendent reality noted by the interpreters of the human situation surveyed in Chapter Four discloses two significant circumstances. First, they overlap considerably, often commenting from different perspectives on the same experiences. Secondly, the experiences themselves are manifold. Variety characterizes not only the observers and their manners of expression, but equally the data which they interpret. Our understanding should be heightened if we now examine some of the main types or kinds of experience in which men and women seem to confront a transcendent dimension in reality. Such experiences include the wonder and awe aroused by awareness of the fathomless depth of their existence, their consciousness of incompleteness and dependence, the search for meaning and wholeness, the call to personal and social responsibility, and the pull of the not-yet or the future. They are often not identified with God at all. However, we may discover that they can quite soundly be regarded as forms of God's unrecognized presence—divine incognitos. They will occupy our attention in the present chapter and the next four.

Sensitive persons frequently become aware of a depth in reality which has no determinable limits and which elicits their wonder and reverence. Serious reflection on our existence prompts the recognition that our human strivings take place in a larger context which constantly affects them. This context is more than our physical environment. It seems to involve something structural in our existence as human beings which nevertheless is not completely identifiable with ourselves or any part of us, and which is not subject to complete comprehension. There are depths within us which cannot be fathomed, defined, or controlled, and which suggest that we participate in a life other and greater than our own. At least a dim awareness of such depths seems to be a universal experience, whether or not it is theistically interpreted.

Kant, it will be recalled, reported that two things filled him with boundless awe, the starry heavens above him and the moral law within him. In broadly similar fashion, the sense of wonder and mystery here referred to may be evoked by two manifestations of the transcendent, which occur in men's relations with the physical world and in their experience of their own personal existence.

Transcendence in the Natural Order

Poets have long sung, with Wordsworth, of a presence in nature which arouses

> . . . a sense sublime,
> Of something far more deeply interfused.

They have been joined by numerous people with only ordinary aesthetic sensitivity who respond with something akin to reverence to the surging power of oceans, the endless expanse of the blue sky, the flaming glow of sunsets, the silence of mountains and forests, the delicate beauty and fragrance of a rose, the marvel of reproduction in plant and animal alike, and the complex processes involved in the ongoing life of their own bodies. Such experiences are not restricted to the romanticists; they are reported by many who know full well that skies are often gray, and who are quite aware of the stark reality of devastating violence in the natural order.

Moreover, many professional scientists find their commitment to the methods of precise research altogether consistent with attitudes of reverence toward, even participation in, the realities discovered in their investigations. Commenting on Otto's account of the holy, William G. Pollard points out that the investigations of the empirical sciences are not lacking in the "overplus of meaning" which the holy essentially involves. This overplus cannot be apprehended or denied according to the canons of sense perception, but all scientists have experiences of great power and worth which do not appear in the conceptual systems that result from their labors. "In the presence of a nuclear reactor in operation," writes Pollard, "a profound sense of mystery and awe comes over me, and all the more intensely the more one knows conceptually about what is taking place in it." [1]

A similar response is reported by Robert S. Cohen, chairman of the department of physics in the College of Liberal Arts and the Graduate School of Boston University. He regards himself as an atheist. Nevertheless, in conversation several years ago he described his position as a kind of "nature mysticism." Feeling a profound sense of being a part of the natural order, he acknowledges that his inquiries into the orderly functioning of physical entities sometimes evoke a sense of wonder and a devotion to the search for truth which are similar to the mood and commitment of some religious believers. Ronald Hepburn goes so far as to maintain that certain "basic experiences" of the Christian are also open to the skeptic. For example, the worshiper's sense of the numinous or the holy finds its counterpart in the impres-

[1] *Physicist and Christian; a Dialogue Between the Communities* (New York: Seabury Press, 1964), pp. 84-96.

sions of awe or "quite inexpressible strangeness" found in the lives of many persons who do not ascribe them to a reality which they would call God.[2] The two types of awareness as experienced are certainly not identical in meaning, since the presence or absence of theistic belief inevitably entails differences in the quality of the event. Yet the skeptic's consciousness of "inexpressible strangeness" may be nevertheless a result of the activity of the God who is present even though to the experient he remains unrecognized.

Contributory to the intimations of transcendence found in man's relation to the natural order is the growing recognition, long over-due, of the interdependence between human beings and their total physical environment. To our great loss, the closeness of this relationship has been largely blotted from view by the widespread Western conception of nature as an antagonist to be conquered—a conception strengthened by the exploitative attitudes and practices of scientific technology. In this respect contemporary men and women have much to learn from simpler cultures which we have done much to suppress, and even to exterminate.

Dorothy Lee observes that the Tikopia, in the Solomon Islands Protectorate, "appear to live in a continuum which includes nature and the divine without defining bounds; where communion is present, not achieved; where merging is a matter of being, not of becoming." She notes similar attitudes among the Hopi, Navaho, and Wintu Indians of North America. The Wintu, for instance, though they lived on land so thick in forest cover that it was difficult to find land open enough for the erection of houses, nevertheless had such respect for nature that they used only dead wood for fuel. An old Wintu woman gave graphic expression to this outlook:

[2] *Christianity and Paradox* (London: C. A. Watts & Co., 1958), pp. 204-8.

The White people never cared for land or deer or bear. When we Indians kill meat, we eat it all up. When we dig roots we make little holes. When we build houses, we make little holes. . . . We shake down acorns and pinenuts. We don't chop down the trees. We only use dead wood. But the White people plow up the ground, pull up the trees, kill everything. The tree says, "Don't, I am sore. Don't hurt me." But they chop it down and cut it up. The spirit of the land hates them. They blast out the trees and stir it up to its depths. They saw up the trees. That hurts them. The Indians never hurt anything, but the White people destroy all. They blast rocks and scatter them on the ground. The rock says "Don't, you are hurting me." But the White people pay no attention. When the Indians use rocks, they take little round ones for their cooking. . . . How can the spirit of the earth like the White man? . . . Everywhere the White man has touched it, it is sore.[3]

There is little need to comment on the polar difference between this sense of close communion between men and nature and the prodigal, wasteful use of natural resources for selfish human ends evident in the denuding of forests, strip mining, and careless destruction of animal species in America, as well as the defoliation, burning, and bombing that have devastated the land of Vietnam.

A valuable by-product of our growing sense of ecological responsibility may be a deepened sensitivity to an activity in our world which transcends, yet is active in, both the natural and the human. Here two words of caution are in order. First, it is important to maintain the unique values of the Hebrew-Christian doctrine of creation, which preserves the ultimacy of God alone, guards the distinction between God and men from pantheistic identification, and keeps clear the freedom and responsibility of human beings. Secondly, the truth of recent theologies of secularization is not to be overlooked in a sentimental worship of

[3] Dorothy Lee, *Freedom and Culture* (Englewood Cliffs, N.J.: Prentice-Hall, 1959), pp. 163-65.

nature. For Christian faith men are released by the gospel from a sacral view of the natural order that makes them subservient to the "many 'gods' and many 'lords' " of which Paul wrote (I Cor. 8:5). Dependent for their acceptance on the grace of God received by faith rather than on the works they perform in either nature or history, they are free to deal with the world in its full worldliness according to their reason and conscience, though as a divine trust. They accept it as an inheritance from God for which they are responsible as mature sons and daughters (Gal. 4:1-9).

Yet there are dangers also in this conception of man's relation to the world. It has sometimes been understood to justify precisely the exploitation of nature which we have noted, as well as to sanction a narrow interpretation of the covenant—old or new—between God and his people. The sensitivity of the American Indians to a sacredness in things may be closer to a genuine experience of the God of all mankind than the nationalistic fervor which used belief in God's gift of Canaan to his chosen people to warrant the wholesale slaughter of the Amalekites and other inhabitants of the Promised Land. The same may be said with respect to the arrogant rationalizations of white Europeans regarding their divine mandate to civilize the "savages" and take their land; of white slave owners who talked sanctimoniously of their responsibility for christianizing the Africans whose lives they controlled; or of the American political and military leaders and churchmen who around 1900 supported American seizure of the Philippines by pious claims of "manifest destiny" and divine authorization for action presumably concerned to safeguard the economic, political, and spiritual well-being of the Filipinos themselves.

What we need is neither the sacral view of primitive cultures, with its merging of nature and the divine and its accompaniment of magical manipulation, nor the separation which divests nature of all religious significance, opening the way to irresponsible human sovereignty and selfish exploitation of our priceless environmental heritage. A deeper wisdom is to recognize our interdependence with the world around us, and the subtle and awesome ways in which our lives are constantly touched by a presence which escapes both our comprehension and our control. Occasionally at least we need to share the mood of the priest turned social revolutionary in Silone's *Bread and Wine*. At a dangerously critical point in his work, he sat at twilight by the roadside,

oppressed by many thoughts. Unseen voices murmured in the distance —shepherds' calls, the barking of dogs and the subdued lowing of the cattle. Mothers called their children from the windows. It was a good time for humility. Man went back to the animal, the animal to the plant, and the plant into the earth. The brook at the bottom of the valley sparkled with stars.[4]

Like George Fox, we must learn "to stand still in the light," becoming thereby aware of a dimension deeper than the shallow pursuit of the values that can be calculated—of technical know-how, material affluence, and power over others. In this awareness we may find ourselves in the presence of God himself.

Transcendence in Personal Existence

The possible theistic significance of the dimension of depth becomes especially evident when we concentrate attention on our human existence as persons—though this can never be divorced from our relations with the natural order. Instead of conceiving the transcendent as that which lies beyond and eludes our experience, we shall be closer to the truth if we affirm its presence within experience. This is the case whether we approach the idea by way of the original meaning of the verb *to transcend,* which referred to an act of crossing or climbing over carried out by

[4] *Bread and Wine,* pp. 294-95.

the human transcender, or adopt the later meaning of the noun *transcendence,* which designates a state of being transcended.

"The deepest use of the vocabulary of transcendence," writes George Frederick Woods, "is to describe the fact of being in existence. To be is to transcend. . . . A personal being knows himself to be existing because he is outstanding above or transcending over what is not." [5] This active transcending seems to extend as well to our experienced relation to much that is. As persons we are aware of ourselves as surmounting our own privacy. But we also have in ordinary life many experiences of being transcended: we know ourselves to be in the presence of other beings which affect our lives in manifold ways. Woods persuasively suggests that such experiences of being ourselves and being in the company of other people, in which we find ourselves both transcending and being transcended, provide the best analogy for our relation to whatever ultimate reality may be.

Further examination of our personal awareness of transcending and being transcended discloses a range and a depth in human existence which elude neat and precise description. The distinctively human contains within itself something which is more than itself. William James reports many instances in human consciousness of "*a sense of reality, a feeling of objective presence, a perception* of what we may call *'something there,'* " deeper and more general than any of the so-called special senses. This sense of reality extends for James to the whole realm of abstract ideas. As time and space permeate all things, so "do abstract and essential goodness, beauty, strength, significance, justice, soak through all things good, strong, significant, and just." Such bodiless and featureless entities can never be directly observed, but they provide the whatness of every particular thing or event. "We grasp all other things by their means," and without them we could not deal with the em-

[5] "The Idea of the Transcendent," *Soundings,* ed. A. R. Vidler (Cambridge: University Press, 1962), p. 56.

pirical world. Inherent in our mental constitution, they are a part of the reality which they enable us to experience.[6]

The contemporary scene offers numerous examples of psychological explorations which lead to conclusions comparable to those of James. Techniques such as group encounter, sensitivity training, psychodrama, and gestalt therapy, as well as Zen and other forms of "transcendental meditation," produce awareness of personal growth into deeper dimensions, participation in a fuller reality than otherwise known, reception of grace or spiritual strength, or the presence of "something more." [7]

Yet such experiences are not limited to groups or individuals who practice specialized disciplines. They occur whenever ordinary people face the mysteries of life and know that at the deepest levels of their being they do not have the last word. Particularly as we confront the critical events of life, such as birth, puberty, decisions regarding sex and marriage, work, illness, aging, and death, we know ourselves to be caught up in processes far greater than ourselves, and over which our control is limited at best. On the negative side, we feel threatened by disease, accident, unemployment, war, loneliness, alienation from other human beings, meaninglessness, uncertainty concerning the future, and the certainty of our own death. On the positive side, our experiences of richest fulfillment seem to come primarily not as our own attainment, but as gifts. We receive more than we achieve.

Langdon Gilkey has with keen discernment called attention to the most direct manifestation of this givenness in the experience of childbirth, especially in the role of the mother. She is the instrument of an activity which far transcends her own. Something ulti-

---

[6] *The Varieties of Religious Experience,* pp. 56-58, 63, 64. Italics by William James.

[7] See Paul W. Pruyser, *A Dynamic Psychology of Religion* (New York: Harper & Row, 1968), pp. 212-13, 227; Michael Murphy, "Education for Transcendence," *Transcendence,* ed. Herbert W. Richardson and Donald R. Cutler, pp. 18-30.

mate works *in* and *through* her, rather than *by* her, to bring forth new life.[8] From this experience all of us receive our being, and something of its inner meaning is open to all who reflect on it with empathy. Here we stand in awe and wonder in the presence of the mysterious power on which we ultimately depend for life and all its values. Whether we know it or not, we stand in the presence of God.

The reference to the transcendent which is discernible in the creation of life itself is similarly apparent in other forms of creation. Creativity in men and women is best understood when related to a deeper creativity in the very nature of reality. The artist, the musical composer, the poet, the dramatist, the architect, the inventor, the author of new ideas in politics or economics is not merely a craftsman utilizing exceptional technical skills. Typically he feels himself to be the vehicle of a creative power, not his own, which wells up within him and surges through him. He does not manage it, but is mastered by it. His insights seem to come to him from a deeper source. His talents, honed perhaps to perfection by disciplined effort, are truly his, and he exercises them in freedom, but he sees them ultimately as gifts. The poem that writes itself in a few minutes and the sonata that rushes into consciousness faster than it can be written down are only extreme instances of an experience which occurs in all genuinely creative action. The urge to create, its realization by human agents, and the awareness of unfulfilled creative potential which beckons us on to further striving are most intelligible when related to a creativity pervading the very structure of reality. We are its carriers, not its originators. Here too we are in the presence of the holy, the *mysterium tremendum* which moves us to wonder, awe, humility, and often gratitude, reverence, devotion, and worship. We

[8] *Naming the Whirlwind,* pp. 317-19.

are confronting a major manifestation of the divine incognito.

Worthy of special note is the fact that manifestations of the transcendent like those cited are acknowledged not only by theists, but also by many persons who regard themselves as humanists and atheists. Even Jean-Paul Sartre finds man's existence marked by a kind of self-transcendence, a "passing beyond" himself. Man exists as he projects or loses himself outside himself in pursuing transcendent goals. His only universe is one of human subjectivity, but subjectivity here refers to everything human, not only to the individual.

This connection between transcendency, as a constituent element of man—not in the sense that God is transcendent, but in the sense of passing beyond—and subjectivity, in the sense that man is not closed in on himself but is always present in a human universe, is what we call existentialist humanism. . . . Man will fulfill himself as man, not in turning toward himself, but in seeking outside himself a goal which is just this liberation, just this particular fulfillment.

Thus the responsibility of each person for his own existence extends beyond his own individuality to include all human beings. Every person chooses himself, but in so doing he chooses all other men and women as well. Every choice which actualizes the person I want to be simultaneously creates an image of man as I think he should be. I choose always what I regard as good, but nothing can be good for me if it is not good for all. Sartre's existential modification of Descartes's *cogito ergo sum* reaches a similar conclusion. The *I* thinks and exists in a social situation, so that the reality which it discovers is more than that of the individual thinker. "Through the *I think* we reach our own self in the presence of others, and the others are just as real to us as our own self. Thus, the man who becomes aware of himself through the *cogito* also perceives all others, and he perceives them as the condition of his own existence." [9]

It may be fairly questioned whether a passing beyond which is really constitutive in human existence can be consistently restricted to a human universe, with no significance whatever for the larger context in which human beings find themselves. It may also be asked whether this limitation offers the best interpretation of human existence as experienced. Nevertheless, Sartre's view must be respected, and our only concern here is to report his recognition of a transcendent element in human life which at least skirts the edges of the depth dimension now under discussion. However, that dimension is clearly affirmed by a variety of other thinkers who stoutly deny belief in any divine reality.

As already noted,[10] the evolutionary humanist Julian Huxley, espousing a "religion without revelation," feels moved to wonder, awe, and reverence by such experiences as an apprehension of sacredness in existence, awareness of inner peace amid distressing circumstances, even a sense of communion with some higher reality. These all relate to aspects of existence which have to do primarily with human destiny and possibilities, but they are referred by Huxley to the operation within men and women of transcendent power.

Like Huxley, J. P. van Praag, chairman of the International Humanist and Ethical Union, stresses the creative possibilities of human beings. Human existence is to be conceived as "human deployment, a development which aims at true humanity." Yet van Praag describes man as the being that realizes itself only by transcending itself. Since human relationships are cosmic as well as natural and social, they can be regarded as having "religious"

---

[9] *Existentialism,* tr. Bernard Frechtman (New York: Philosophical Library, 1947), pp. 59-60, 20, 44.
[10] Above, p. 37.

meaning. Humanism is "a conviction of life by which man with the totality of his faculties is connected with the totality of his conditions of existence." [11]

This religious meaning receives more emphasis in the thought of William Hamilton, in spite of the vehemence of his proclamation that God is dead. Hamilton insists that the death-of-God theology does not ignore or deny the mysterious, the holy, or even the transcendent in human life. However, it cannot give the name God to such experiences, seeking rather to find and celebrate them amid the demands and choices of ordinary life in the world, where man is able through science and technology to control nature for his own ends. [12]

Especially noteworthy—in view of the traditional Marxist rejection of religion as a result of economic exploitation which will die of itself when the classless society is achieved—are recent statements by Marxist thinkers which in various ways recognize the impact on finite men and women of more ultimate questions. Thus the Jugoslav Branko Bosnjak, in a discussion at the meeting of the *Paulus-Gesellschaft* in Salzburg in 1965, held that religious faith is a mode of existence which roots in human consciousness of the reality of death. In the deepest sense man is a tragic being because he is aware of his mortality. As the wish for eternity which is the antithesis of death, religion can exist in any social system, and will survive as long as human beings are moved by anxiety in relation to death and the corresponding desire for eternity. "We find ourselves confronting the supreme mystery because we do not know why there is something and not nothing." [13]

At the same gathering another Marxist, Cesare Luporini of the

[11] *Humanism* (Utrecht: International Humanist and Ethical Union, 1957), pp. 18-21.

[12] "The Death of God," *Playboy,* August, 1966, pp. 137-39.

[13] *Christentum und Marxismus—heute,* ed. Erich Kellner (Wien, Frankfurt, Zürich: Europa Verlag, 1966), pp. 117-18.

University of Florence, declared that it would be foolish for Marxists to deny the presence of mystery in reality. This acknowledgment, along with his decreased emphasis on the mythical element in religion, led him to speak of the future possibility of an objective rapprochement between believers and unbelievers.[14]

Roger Garaudy of Paris goes farther than either Bosnjak or Luporini to identify himself with belief in the transcendent. Marxism, he asserts, owes much to Christianity for its contribution to "the exploration of the two essential dimensions of man: subjectivity and transcendence." He recognizes, of course, the substantial difference between Christian and Marxist conceptions of transcendence. For the Christian, transcendence is "the act of God who comes toward him and summons him," whereas for the Marxist it is "a dimension of man's activity which goes out of itself toward its far-off being." However, for the latter as well as the former, it is an aspect of human existence which lies deeper than all surface appearances and, in ways which defy neat programming, opens up as yet unrealized possibilities in human existence.[15]

This meaning of the transcendent has been eloquently formulated in the philosophy of Ernst Bloch. Though Bloch is a Marxist and an avowed atheist, he celebrates in all his writings the dynamic, creative character of reality. The God he rejects is the static, timeless, absolute sovereign of an already finished world, who requires and guarantees the fulfillment of his arbitrary will and denies all independent initiative to his human subjects, from whom he exacts unquestioning trust and obedience. For such religion the outcome is already determined, and there can be no genuine movement forward and no really open future.

For Bloch, on the contrary, "the real is process"; it proceeds on a moving, changing front toward a possible but not yet deter-

---

[14] *Ibid.*, p. 141.
[15] *From Anathema to Dialogue* (New York: Herder and Herder, 1966), pp. 112, 92.

mined future. Deeply rooted in the nature of things is the urge to realize the not-yet, the latent possibilities of existence. Reality exhibits "a transcending without heavenly transcendence." Man is on a risky pilgrimage in which he is summoned to transcend every present, but without the guarantee of a transcendent reality already complete. Before him beckons the potential for the genuinely new, which Bloch finds best portrayed as the new heaven and the new earth of the prophets and the New Testament writers. The ground of all unfixed possibilities is "matter." But Bloch's materialism is dialectical, not mechanistic. He conceives matter dynamically and qualitatively, as the source of an advancing, open-ended process. As its cognate *mater* suggests, it is the ultimate matrix of all objectively real possibilities, the substratum of the movement and novelty of existence, the fruitful womb from which man's future and its own are born. Its potentialities are inexhaustible.[16]

Bloch's revolutionary humanism asserts emphatically the indispensability of the work of socialized man, which alone can translate possibility into reality. No less strongly he affirms the ultimacy of the world process which provides the necessary basis for the realization of the possible. To this process he credits powers and activities which much Christian theism ascribes to divine agency. His name for the ultimate is matter rather than God—a preference for which traditional Christian dogma bears no small share of responsibility—but in the depths of reality he finds at work a power no less creative and redemptive than that of the God proclaimed in authentic Christian worship.

[16] *Das Prinzip Hoffnung* (Frankfurt am Main: Suhrkamp Verlag, 1969), pp. 225, 284-85, 287-88, 1413, 1522, 1524, 1566, 1625-27; *Tübinger Einleitung in die Philosophie* (Frankfurt am Main: Suhrkamp Verlag, 1963-1964), I, ˙175-76, 185-86; II, 176-79; *Philosophische Grundfragen; Zur Ontologie des Noch-Nicht-Seins* (Frankfurt am Main: Suhrkamp Verlag, 1961), pp. 16-18, 25-39; *Dokumente der Paulus-Gesellschaft*, ed. Erich Kellner, XII, 112, 117-19.

Looking back now on the two pathways followed, we find them leading in the same direction. Alike in our experience of the physical order and in our own historical existence as persons, we human beings confront a reality that is other and deeper than ourselves. Impinging on our lives at every point is an activity which in subtle and powerful ways affects our own, and which we can neither fully comprehend nor control. An account of human experience which omits this dimension is flat and thin, incapable of depicting adequately the real world we know. Something transcendent seems to be as intimately involved in our total human situation as is the third dimension in our apprehension of physical objects. A space conceived in terms of plane surfaces alone lacks real body and substance. Only when it is at least three-dimensional is it the space investigated by geometry and physics and experienced in daily life, and only when the dimension of time is added does adequate understanding become possible.

Do we not have here a sound clue to any adequate interpretation of our experience as a whole? In the larger enterprise, too, our inquiry will be superficial if it does not take account of the dimension of more-than-human depth and dynamic movement. The name we give to this dimension may not matter very much, but it is integral to human existence, and it is one aspect at least of what theistic faith calls God.

6 HUMAN DEPENDENCE

nseparable from our awareness of the depth in our experience of reality is the consciousness of receiving our existence from something beyond ourselves. We are neither self-originating nor self-sustaining. We are here through no decision or action of our own, but as a result of events with which we had nothing whatever to do. Once we are given our being, we are dependent for what it becomes on factors which to a considerable extent are beyond our control.

Schleiermacher no doubt claimed too much when he declared that the common and distinguishing element in all diverse expressions of religion is "the feeling of absolute dependence." Religion involves much more than emotion, even an emotion so sweeping as a consciousness of being utterly dependent. Nevertheless, in citing the experience of dependence Schleiermacher did quite rightly call attention to *one* characteristic feature of the religious attitude. In another respect we may go beyond him to point out that an awareness of dependence is a universal characteristic of a self-conscious response to the human situation—whether the attitude may be properly described as religious or not.

In this awareness are intimations of transcendence which deserve further examination. Three forms of the experience are discernible: (1) our dependence on forces beyond ourselves for physical existence; (2) the limited, finite, conditioned nature of our lives; and (3) our incompleteness, which moves us to reach out beyond ourselves for a fulfillment which eludes our own powers.

Contingency

All thoughtful persons are aware, however dimly, of being related to an objective world which is other and more than themselves as subjects, taken either individually or collectively. We find ourselves confronting a reality that was obviously there before we came on the scene. We encounter objects, other persons, and events, conscious of being acted on by them but without any awareness of responsibility for their existence.[1] Moreover, the total reality of what we encounter is of crucial importance to us. Without it we could not *be*. Without any determining choice on our part we find ourselves in a world that does not depend on us, but on which we depend for our very being and its continuance.

On reflection, however, we discover that our dependence has a positive as well as a negative facet. On the one hand, we know ourselves to be creatures threatened with nothingness; but on the other, the reality on which we depend gives us life and a measure of freedom—gifts that are renewed in each moment. That is, both major meanings of the word *depend* are applicable. Our existence is contingent on the reality that we confront, but it also relies on it, places confidence in it, trusts it. The being we enjoy is not its own ground, but it does have a ground which can be counted on. If we are threatened, we are also supported. All that we are, the whole intricate structure of relationships with other persons and the natural order, would be nonexistent apart from the activity of

[1] See John E. Smith, *Experience and God,* p. 13.

something other than ourselves. Yet that other is dependable and trustworthy, so that our existence is not only hazardous but hopeful.

This two-faceted sense of dependence on an order that transcends both individuals and human society as a whole seems to be a universal human experience. When it is related to other aspects of our human encounter with reality it may be reasonably interpreted as the activity of what theistic faith calls God. The sheer contingency of our creaturely existence points us toward something which is not contingent, an ultimate reality which merits our trust even as it arouses our trepidation.

Limitation

One July morning, as I was reflecting on the content and construction of this chapter, my attention was attracted to two robins searching for food on the lawn. One was a full-sized female; the other, smaller, had the speckled breast which identified it as a fledgling in the process of learning from its mother how to fend for itself. The baby robin hopped toward the small garden on the edge of the grass, perhaps attracted by the promise of insects in the lush, thick growth of the tomato plants, only to have its advance suddenly barred by the almost invisible mesh wire that had been erected earlier to thwart the rabbits which had begun to eat the young plants. The frustration and perplexity of the young bird could hardly have been more evident. He hopped slowly along the barrier, stopping occasionally for a futile attempt to penetrate it, then disappeared around the corner of the tomato patch to continue his efforts. He could understand neither what it was that hindered him nor what might lie beyond. He did experience the stern reality of an impassable frontier and the vague awareness of something on the other side.

In the predicament of that questing robin I saw myself and my fellow human beings. We, too, confront on all sides limits which we can neither comprehend nor penetrate—finitude, transitoriness, mortality, unsurmountable restrictions of both knowledge and power. Though we are conditioned by them, there seems to be something about them which, at least in its impact on us, is unconditioned. John A. T. Robinson accurately describes our experience when he speaks of "the unconditional" which "forms the living frontier, in and out, of every aspect of man's being, of every particle of the universe." [2] We are aware of an ultimate limit which conditions us in all directions, a horizon beyond which we cannot go, not so much because it recedes as we advance but because we lack equipment for the journey. The contingent, relative reality which we know in part confronts us against the background of an absolute, enduring ultimate which is its source. The confrontation stirs within us an awareness both of our own limitations and of the power and importance for our lives of what lies beyond.

Some such account of our human situation would probably win the general acceptance of most persons, whether they interpret it religiously or nonreligiously. For example, Roger Garaudy, influential French Marxist, holds that Marxist humanism is no less interested than theism in "the questions men ask about the meaning of their life and death, about the problem of their origin and their end, about the demands of their thought and their heart." The dialectic of finite and infinite is a concrete reality for all human beings. Marxists no less than Christians experience the inadequacy of all partial and relative being; they confront the same exigency and feel the same tension concerning the future.

Sharp differences arise, of course, over the significance of such experiences for the nature of the reality beyond the limits. Garaudy rejects decisively what he regards as the dogmatism, the definitive-

[2] *Exploration into God* (Stanford: Stanford University Press, 1967), pp. 11, 68-69.

ness, and the illusoriness of the answers given by theistic faith. Marxism has no quarrel with the questions raised or even the authentic aspiration which evokes the answers, but it cannot accept the mythical and alienated notions of transcendence which it finds in the Christian response. Our thirst does not demonstrate the existence of the spring that satisfies it. Marxism is a critical philosophy, and therefore cannot transform questions into answers, alienation into promise, exigency into presence.

We can live this exigency, and we can set it out, but we cannot conceive it, name it or expect it. Even less can we hypostasize it under the name of transcendence. Regarding this totality, this absolute, I can say everything except: It is. For what it is is always deferred and growing, like man himself.

If we want to give it a name, the name will not be that of God, for it is impossible to conceive of a God who is always in process of making himself, in process of being born.[3]

The position here set forth as critical deserves an equally critical response. The distinction between questions and answers is valid and clarifying, and obviously the former do not imply or require the latter. On the negative side, however, two observations need to be made. First, in Garaudy's aversion to traditional absolutistic theism he overlooks the possibility of a synthesis of becoming and being in the ultimate. There is no a priori reason why change must be excluded from transcendent reality any more than it is from the human existence which is Garaudy's model. Process theologians, personalistic idealists, and evolutionary thinkers like Teilhard de Chardin are representative of a considerable number of contemporary and historical thinkers whose theistic metaphysics yields nothing to Marxism in its affirmation of dynamism and movement.

Secondly, Garaudy undermines his claim to a critical stance by

[3] *From Anathema to Dialogue*, pp. 88-95.

assuming that the existential questions support his own answers. Is not Marxism just as "dogmatic" as Christianity if it categorically denies the presence and promise of God? Garaudy makes "the humble admission that we cannot say: I know." He is not humble, however, in his assertion of negative knowledge. He describes as "simple awareness of our condition" that "the whole of our history and its significance is played out within man's intelligence, heart and will, and nowhere else." [4] Here Garaudy merely begs the question, uncritically leaping from the given reality of difficulties and possibilities in our human situation to atheistic conclusions. Moreover, when he maintains that Marxist atheism takes away from men only "the illusion of certainty," he forgets that Christian faith is not a claim to certainty but an act of trust, and that Marxism may be guilty of cherishing an illusion of *negative* certainty.

Basically, we are dealing with divergent interpretations of the same empirical data. One is not inherently more self-assured or dogmatic than the other, and neither can be soundly held to be equivalent to the condition which they seek to interpret. Both are attempts to offer intelligible accounts of the human situation. Neither yields final certainty, and both involve faith, the validity of which cannot be demonstrated.

Are there, then, any conclusions which are warranted or suggested by the conditionedness of human existence? Clearly the presence of a boundary in itself says nothing as to the nature of what lies beyond it. However, a boundary is an aspect of a total situation as we experience it, and that situation as a whole provides the only data we have in our search for truth. Remembering the closeness of the subject-object relationship, if we consider the human subject who knows himself conditioned together with the nature of the limitations which he experiences, we may be able

[4] *Ibid.*, p. 95.

to form some defensible judgments concerning the reality which encompasses us.

Hegel has observed that to experience a limit is in some sense also to transcend it, since we could hardly know it as a limit unless there was in us some aim frustrated by its presence and an image of the real in which the frustration might be overcome. Ernst Bloch likewise declares that to the degree that we notice the existence of limits we have already transcended them. This transcending appears as boredom, as the absence of salvation (*Unheil*), or as reaching out toward something not in time. Imperfection, for example, is all around us, yet in Bloch's view the idea of perfection is innate, a substitute for something which is *not yet* there—but which may become real.[5]

With very different metaphysical premises Martin Heidegger reaches somewhat similar conclusions, which also appear with theistic overtones in a number of contemporary Christian theologians. In Heidegger's view man's awareness of the threat of nonbeing, as in the negation or absence of being which he experiences in anxiety, occasions a disclosure of being—both his own being-there (*Dasein*) and the Being in all finite beings.[6]

Paul Tillich describes the confrontation with the threat of nonbeing in terms of "ontological shock," in which the mind reaches its boundary and is thrown off balance, "shaken in its structure." However, what is experienced is "the negative side of the mystery of being—its abysmal element." Thus the experience of the shock of nonbeing actually produces a consciousness of the power of being. Indeed, Tillich regards this negative element as necessary for revelation, since without it mystery would not be mysterious. Without Isaiah's awareness of being "undone" his vision of God

---

[5] *Dokumente der Paulus-Gesellschaft,* ed. Erich Kellner, XII, 114.

[6] *An Introduction to Metaphysics,* tr. Ralph Manheim (New Haven: Yale University Press, 1959), Chap. 1.

would have been impossible. Apart from "the dark night of the soul" the mystic could not experience the mystery of the ground of being.[7]

For Rudolf Bultmann, too, our knowledge of the limits we face has important positive implications. All human beings are conscious of their finitude, and of the uncanniness and enigmatic nature of their lives. This awareness constitutes a kind of "pre-understanding" which is an aspect of the human question concerning God. Out of the consciousness of our temporality and transitoriness arises talk of something eternal and transcendent. Initially, writes Bultmann, knowledge about God is "*a knowledge which man has about himself and his finitude, and God is reckoned to be the power which breaks through this finitude of man and thereby raises him up to his real nature.* [8]

Admittedly, there is nothing self-validating about a theistic response to a sense of finitude or the threat of nonbeing. Nevertheless, both the situation and the response reflect the ontological structure of human existence and its place in the universe. As Wolfhart Pannenberg observes, "man is essentially referred to infinity but is never already infinite in himself." [9] This circumstance must be taken with full seriousness as we try to form sound judgments concerning the reality which encompasses us. Moreover, the human effort to transcend finitude often yields positive results. Many men and women are impelled by anxiety, emptiness, or the threat of nothingness to search for something unconditioned or ultimate which imparts stability and worth to their existence. Frequently this search leads to indisputable experi-

[7] *Systematic Theology,* I (Chicago: University of Chicago Press, 1951), 110, 113, 186.

[8] *Glauben und Verstehen; Gesammelte Aufsätze,* IV (Tübingen: J. C. B. Mohr [Paul Siebeck], 1965), 120-21, n. 27; *Essays Philosophical and Theological* (New York: The Macmillan Co., 1955), pp. 94-98.

[9] *Basic Questions in Theology,* II (Philadelphia: Fortress Press, 1971), 191.

ences of support, acceptance, creativity, beauty, and hope. Whatever else reality may ultimately be, it includes experiences like these. The total dialectical process which makes them possible may be soundly regarded as a form of the unrecognized activity of God.

Incompleteness

A third form of the experience of dependence is our awareness of incompleteness and inadequacy. In greater or less degree all human beings are conscious of the fragmentary, unconsummated character of their existence. When analyzed, this consciousness seems to include three aspects. (1) We recognize in ourselves potentialities for growth or attainment beyond the level so far realized. There is a certain open-endedness in persons which encourages belief in the possibility of a future not wholly determined by the past. (2) We feel an inward pressure to actualize our potentialities, to become more, other, or better than we are. We have aspirations which outrun our accomplishments, a reach which exceeds our grasp. (3) We are therefore dissatisfied with what we are. Disturbed by the gap between the potential and the actual, we look for some way to bridge it. We are unhappy with the shallowness, the pettiness, the failure, or the wrongness of our present existence, and feel the need to overcome it. Aware of a brokenness in our relations with other persons and with the total milieu of our lives, we want to be healed and made whole. In the broadest sense, we long for salvation, whether it entails the restoration of a lost harmony or the fulfillment of goals not yet achieved.

This kind of experience is by no means limited to religious believers. For example, though Roger Garaudy does not share the belief in "the superhuman," man's consciousness of the infinite, which he finds in Christianity, he accepts the genuineness of the experience which provides the basis for this belief: all human beings are aware of their incompleteness and their as yet unrealized possibilities which they are summoned to fulfill. Marxists observe a "tension towards the future" which they take to be characteristic of human life.[10] Thus they agree with Christians in affirming the reality of a self-transcending quality in human existence.

This awareness of incompleteness, this tension thrusting us toward the future is not adequately accounted for within the framework of our own human history alone. It suggests something constitutive in our relation to the larger reality which begets, sustains, and challenges us. In experiencing the self-transcending quality of our own lives we encounter an activity in reality itself which transcends all finite existence.

At least partial confirmation of this judgment is found in the empirical fact that our struggle toward greater completeness depends at every point not only on our own endeavor, but on factors other than ourselves. The very possibility of finding in our complex relationships with the world and with other persons the fulfillment of our own potential is grounded in an Other, or others. In the process we draw on manifold resources which we do not ourselves provide—talents which are ours by endowment rather than achievement, the physical order with its complex life-sustaining operations, and the past and present contributions of other people. It was acute observation of our actual condition which prompted the apostle Paul to ask the Corinthian Christians, "What have you that you did not receive? If then you received it, why do you boast as if it were not a gift?" (I Cor. 4:7.)

Furthermore, our fullest self-realization is conditioned on our consciously and positively relating ourselves to this complex Other

---

[10] *Christentum und Marxismus—heute,* ed. Erich Kellner, p. 77; *From Anathema to Dialogue,* p. 61.

in the structure of reality as we encounter it. Only as we devote ourselves to an object of supreme worth beyond ourselves can we achieve the fulfillment of our selfhood. Without this transcendent reference, we become self-centered and sterile, incapable of actualizing our potentialities. With it, however, we may move toward the actualization of our greatest good. The experience of large numbers of persons witnesses to the practical availability of a dynamic process which upholds and advances our best efforts. The creativity which precedes and calls forth our endeavors responds to our commitment with powerful support. What historic Christian faith has called grace is not a figment of the pious imagination, but an empirical reality. It is no less real because human beings sometimes give it the wrong name, or mistakenly refer it to their own powers.

The various lines of investigation pursued in this chapter lead to the same conclusion: Our existence as a whole remains unintelligible unless we include the dimension of transcendence disclosed by our experience of dependence. The contingency, limitation, and incompleteness of human life refer it to an ultimate ground which is other and greater than itself. On it we depend for both existence and fulfillment. Confronting it, the theist acknowledges the living presence of God and responds in gratitude and devotion. In full respect for those who interpret their situation differently, he may justly hold that they too are sustained by the power and love of one who remains for them unrecognized.

7 THE SEARCH FOR MEANING
AND WHOLENESS

Meaning

Lewis Mumford has distinguished between two kinds of questions faced by human beings: the "little" ones which can be definitely answered; and the larger and profounder ones which concern the basic meaning of existence. The former have an important practical function, but they gain their full significance only when seen in a larger context. "Nothing can be settled until everything is settled. The first step in the re-education of man is for him to come to terms with his ultimate destiny." [1]

There is convincing evidence in support of Mumford's judgment. The historical manifestations of religion, widely divergent though they have been in their beliefs, rituals, and practices, have had in common a serious and insistent quest for meaning. The same concern is apparent in human beings today, whether or not they regard it as religious. For example, the sociologist Robert N. Bellah observes in contemporary society an intense search for personal authenticity, a deep preoccupation with innerness or genuineness of personal experience, along with suspicion toward outward

[1] *The Universal God,* ed. C. H. Voss (Cleveland: World Publishing Co., 1953), p. 51.

authority. Men and women are at least as much concerned with the exploration of "inner space" as with probing the far reaches of our solar system and beyond. For increasing numbers of people naïve literalism in religion has become impossible, but the "ultimate questions about the meaning of life are asked as insistently, perhaps more insistently than ever." [2]

Indeed, a major characteristic of our existence is its questionableness. Reality as it confronts us is interrogative. Not only to "the man" in Genesis 3:9, but to every man and woman in every generation the question is put, "Where are you?" and none can evade it. Fundamental to all the smaller questions is the query concerning our real identity and the values which should claim our allegiance. It comes to us in different forms and with varying degrees of clarity, but sooner or later it must be answered: Who are you? What does it mean for you to be a person? What are you for? What are you doing? Whither are you headed? What do you want to become? What is your responsibility to your fellows? At the heart of all such questions is the concern of those who ask them for some awareness that their existence may count for something, that the activities which absorb their energies may be worthful, that their lives may have genuine value for themselves and others.

So important is this "will-to-meaning" that Viktor Frankl regards it as the characteristic most distinctive in human beings; animals never worry about the meaning of their existence. According to Frankl persons live in three dimensions: the somatic, the mental, and the spiritual. The primary feature of the spiritual dimension is the search for meaning. That which "most deeply inspires man" is "the innate desire to give as much meaning as possible to one's life, to actualize as many values as possible." What is sought, however, is not meaning in life in general, but

_____
[2] *Beyond Belief*, p. 227.

meaning in the particular life of the individual at a particular time and place—meaning in *my* life, in *my* situation. In short, meaning is existential; it differs from person to person, day to day, and hour to hour. Each person is questioned or addressed by life in each context. He is called on to decide what he should do, what his task or mission is, in this particular moment.

Whether the questions we raise concerning our own meaning are considered specifically or as a whole, they can hardly be ignored in our efforts to interpret the reality which encompasses and confronts us. They arise in our commerce with reality, and something in our relation to it prompts us to raise them. The fact that we do raise them—that we are impelled to seek meaning —sheds important light on the character of reality. Indeed, do not our questions point to the presence at the heart of human life of one who is himself the answer? Ultimately they are a form of our search for God, a search which is undertaken because of our underlying relation to him and at least a dim awareness on our part as to who he is. Though he often remains incognito, it is he who prompts the questions and he alone who adequately resolves them.[3] As Augustine put it in looking back on his own long quest, we are made for God, and the restlessness which ends only in communion with him is an expression of his action in seeking us.

Gordon W. Allport tells a Muslim legend which conveys the same truth with appealing simplicity. A dervish was tempted by the devil to cease praying because Allah did not answer, "Here am I." But then the prophet Khadir brought to the dervish in a vision Allah's message: "Was it not J who summoned thee to my

---

[3] This conception that the question raised by human existence is grounded in the answer which is God himself appears in contemporary theologians as diverse as Karl Barth, Rudolf Bultmann, Gerhard Ebeling, Paul Tillich, Helmut Gollwitzer, Wolfhart Pannenberg, and Langdon Gilkey.

service? Did I not make thee busy with my name? Thy calling 'Allah' was my 'Here am I.' " [4]

Here an urgent word of caution is in order. The affirmation that God himself is at the root of our quest for meaning must not lead us to forget that many persons seek meaning in self-defeating or dangerously anti-social ways, such as drug "trips," "dropping out" of society, hijacking planes, or attempting assassinations of important public figures. Arthur Bremer, who shot Governor George Wallace at a political rally in Laurel, Maryland in March, 1972, revealed his low self-estimate when he wrote in his diary, "My future is small, my past an insult to any human being." But apparently he hoped to win both distinction and publicity and offset his failures by one act which remained within his power. While stalking Richard Nixon during the President's visit to Ottawa he wrote, "This will be one of the most closely read pages since the Scrolls in those caves. . . . I'm as important as the start of World War I. . . . I am a Hamlet. . . . I hope my death makes more sense than my life." [5]

Nor do we dare overlook the fact that for millions of others who do not go to such bizarre extremes the quest for meaning is still futile. Meaninglessness, emptiness, boredom, despair—these are the grim realities they know. If their call for help is already the "Here am I" of Allah or God, they remain tragically unaware of the fact. In our ultimate interpretation of existence, negative circumstances like these must be faced with utter realism.

In the present context we are concerned mainly to call attention to the implications of the search itself. Yet even the experience of meaninglessness involves the assumption that life claims to be significant: some belief in meaning or its possibility is the point of reference. Paul Tillich has penetratingly commented that

---

[4] *The Individual and His Religion* (New York: The Macmillan Co., 1951), p. 136.

[5] *Newsweek,* August 14, 1972, pp. 22, 23.

even doubt and despair express the meaning in which the doubter and the desperate are still living. "This unconditioned seriousness is the expression of the presence of the divine in the experience of their separation from it." [6]

Moreover, evidence is widespread that meaning can be found, sometimes even in the most forbidding circumstances. Peculiarly relevant in this connection are the conclusions drawn by Viktor Frankl from his experience in Nazi concentration camps, where the options were drastically limited. He points out that we are required to respond differently in different situations; sometimes by action, sometimes by contemplation, sometimes by suffering. If the last is the case, we can find a unique opportunity in the way in which we bear suffering. Here our concern is not to gain pleasure or avoid pain, but to see meaning in our lives. As Nietzsche saw, "He who has a *why* to live for can bear with almost any *how*."

Even amid the brutal conditions of life in concentration camps men still had some choices. If all other avenues were closed, the values which Frankl calls attitudinal were still realizable. "Everything can be taken from a man but one thing: the last of the human freedoms—to choose one's attitude in any given set of circumstances, to choose one's way." Every day offered opportunity for the prisoner to decide whether he would or would not submit to the powers which threatened to rob him of his inner freedom, his selfhood. The kind of person he became depended not on camp influences alone, but on his own inward decision. There were enough examples, some heroic, to show that irritability could be controlled and apathy overcome. Many individuals preserved a vestige of spiritual freedom and independence of mind. Some went through the huts comforting other prisoners, sometimes giving away their last crust of bread. Two would-be suicides

[6] *The Protestant Era* (Chicago: University of Chicago Press, 1948), pp. xi-xii.

found meaning in the awareness of something still expected of them which they alone could provide. In one case a beloved child in another country awaited in hope the return of the father who was irreplaceable in his affections. In the other a series of scientific books depended for completion on the specialized capacities of the one who had begun the project. A person who becomes conscious of such responsibilities cannot willingly throw away his life. Knowing the *why* of his existence, he can endure almost any *how*. Fundamentally, concludes Frankl, even under extreme restrictions and sufferings a person can still decide what is to become of him, mentally and spiritually. No one can take away from him his own dignity.[7]

No more vivid illustration of the truth of Frankl's conviction could be found than the attitude of Dan Berrigan when seized by the FBI in November, 1969. Father Berrigan, a Jesuit priest, had previously been sentenced to three years' imprisonment for pouring blood on draft files in Catonsville, Maryland. He then disappeared, and for four months, shielded by many friends, he eluded capture by America's top law-enforcement agency. Finally he was apprehended outside the home of William Stringfellow on Block Island by FBI agents posing as bird watchers. Without weapons, he came out to meet the armed officers of the law, who quickly manacled his wrists. The photograph of Father Dan and an unnamed captor leaving the scene, widely circulated in the press, speaks volumes about the real meaning of freedom. The officer's countenance betrays no satisfaction in the thought of duty fulfilled; instead, his dark frown and the grim set of his jaw hint that he is caught in a structure which inhibits his achievement of any genuine individuality. In contrast, Berrigan's face is covered with a broad smile, and the seeming buoyancy of his gait testifies to the inner joy of one who has found release in

[7] *Man's Search for Meaning*, pp. 103-7, 121, 126-27; *The Doctor and the Soul*, pp. xii-xiii. See above, pp. 62-65.

being loyal to his deepest convictions. In this event the captor is imprisoned, the captive liberated; the free is bound and the bound free. There was nothing shallow about Dan Berrigan's perception of his predicament as he went off to jail. He served twenty-seven months in Danbury before being paroled. His health was so undermined that he nearly died. Yet no outward circumstances could rob him of his faith or his integrity, and he emerged to plunge again into the antiwar activities which spring from his commitment to the value and sanctity of human life.

In ordinary circumstances there is much less external interference with the possibilities for significant and worthy existence than for either Viktor Frankl during World War II or Daniel Berrigan from 1969 to 1972. We dare never gloss over the extent or intensity of human suffering or ignore the "lives of quiet desperation" which are far more numerous than Emerson could have anticipated. Yet men, women, and children are finding meaning and purpose in their daily existence; often their lives are enriched by experiences of beauty, truth, love, wonder, and trust which exceed their highest expectations. Both the impulse to search for meaning and the experience of finding it point beyond themselves to the environing reality which makes them possible. Whether recognized as such or not, they may be rightly regarded as one form of the active presence of God.

Wholeness

The quest for meaning leads unavoidably to concern for the attainment of unity and wholeness in human existence. This is true partly because the query, "How can I become whole?" is one of the ultimate questions raised by all who seek a sense of personal significance. It is true also because the questions we ask about our identity, values, and destiny cannot be answered in isolation from one another or apart from consideration of the total context of our lives, which bears directly on them. The same circumstances which give rise to questions of meaning confront us just as urgently with the problems of isolation and fragmentariness, and unless we can achieve some measure of integration the search for meaning will be fruitless. Partial meanings are inevitably specious and unstable. Somehow they must be interrelated in a total system of meaning—though not a rigid one—which takes account of all our experience, if meaninglessness is to be overcome.

The need for wholeness is perennial. World history and literature make plain that men and women have always been troubled by guilt, self-estrangement, hostility, and misunderstanding in their relations with other persons, and by a consciousness of being out of harmony with some deeper reality. They have always needed integration within themselves and reconciliation with society and the world. But fragmentation has multiplied in recent decades.

A host of writers have called attention to the divisions in Western culture related to the increasing domination of scientific technology: competing specializations; the frequent divorce of knowledge from other values; pursuit of highly sophisticated research in disregard of its implications for the ethical quality of human life; wasteful and irresponsible use, even destruction, of natural resources without regard for the environment as a whole or the welfare of future generations. It is now almost trite to lament the spread of alienation and polarization in American society, but it is there for all to see in the deep-seated antagonisms between conservatives and liberals, blacks and whites, hawks and doves, affluent and poor. Wide gaps appear alike in the relations between generations and in the credibility of individuals and political groups. A nation historically dedicated to the freedom, self-determination, and well-being of peoples found itself unleashing in Vietnam its incredibly devastating might, killing, maiming, and making homeless many hundreds of thousands of peasants in order to maintain in power an aristocratic military clique which ruthlessly suppresses freedom. All this finds its counterpart in the widening and heightening of tension, alienation, and conflict within individuals.

The reconciliation of our divisions requires, among other things, a broader perspective and a more universal object of devotion. Neither our private selves nor our limited groups, whether social, ethnic, national, or religious, offer a sufficiently wide frame of reference. Nor does even humanity itself. Ultimately human life is part of a far larger reality, and no part of that reality can be blocked out or overlooked if we are to attain mental or spiritual health. To become whole persons at home in our world we must somehow become harmoniously related to the whole to which we belong. "The whole," moreover, cannot be limited to space or present experience. Human life emerges out of the remote past and moves forward into the indefinite future, and some of our profoundest questions have to do with our relation to time and eternity. In one way or another we must all come to terms with the mystery of our own future, and for the more thoughtful among us this includes the problem of the destiny of society.

Historically, the search for wholeness in human existence has found expression chiefly in the religious life of mankind. The religious concern, says Tillich, is "ultimate, unconditioned, total, and infinite." [8] Many of the major religious symbols are efforts to grasp reality as a whole. As Robert Bellah has noted, terms like God, Being, Life, and Nothingness are not symbols for particular empirical realities, but relational symbols which seek to overcome the "dichotomies of ordinary conceptualization and bring together the coherence of the whole of experience." [9] Allport

[8] *Systematic Theology,* I, 12.
[9] *Beyond Belief,* p. 202.

expresses the same truth more personally and concretely when he describes the religion of an individual as "his ultimate attempt to enlarge and to complete his own personality by finding the supreme context in which he rightly belongs." [10]

In its historical and contemporary manifestations religion exhibits an almost bewildering variety. However, in most of its forms it aims to overcome fragmentation and the threat of chaos by relating persons to a cosmic order or a holistic activity in reality which provides a creative and redemptive center of ultimate meaning. As one aspect of its concern for the whole, it calls on its practitioners to see their lives not merely in terms of the moment, but in the perspective of eternity.

In considerable measure the religious quest has succeeded in its search for ultimate unity. Whether men discover a wholeness which characterizes the objective world or simply project their own order on the totality of being, reality as they experience it religiously is a whole to which they can relate themselves significantly, finding therein integrity and fulfillment. Characteristic of religious experience, concludes William James after surveying many of its varieties, is the individual's sense of continuity with "a wider self through which saving experiences come." [11] Often the resulting awareness is dim, yet it is sufficient. Like Wallace Stevens, perhaps,

> We feel the obscurity of an order, a whole,
> A knowledge, that which arranged the rendezvous,
>
> Within its vital boundary, in the mind.
> We say God and the imagination are one . . .
> How high that highest candle lights the dark.

[10] *The Individual and His Religion,* p. 142.
[11] *Varieties of Religious Experience,* p. 515.

> Out of this same light, out of the central mind,
> We make a dwelling in the evening air,
> In which being there together is enough.[12]

The holistic thrust of religious beliefs and practices has also had important social and cultural consequences. The negative influences of traditional and authoritarian religion on scientific inquiry in Europe are well known. Still widely unrecognized, unfortunately, is the decisive role played by Jewish-Christian monotheism in paving the way for the modern scientific enterprise and its world-shaking discoveries. It is not accidental that scientific research as developed in recent centuries originated and has reached its highest development in the West, where nature has been seen as the creation of one wise God whose rational laws, universally valid, provide the basic structure of a dependable order.

Sociologists like Peter L. Berger have pointed out that the "sacred canopy" of religion has also tended to confer on social institutions "an ultimately valid ontological status" by locating them within a cosmic frame of reference.[13] For this reason religion has often served as a conservative agent in society, enabling corrupt as well as beneficial institutional arrangements to claim ultimate divine sanction. It is readily overlooked, however, that prophetic religion likewise has grounded its demands for justice and radical personal and social change in the righteous will of one universal God.

Like our questions regarding meaning, our concern for wholeness must be taken into account as we try to interpret the character of reality. May not the question, "How can I be made whole?" be prompted by the presence in the ground of our existence of

[12] *Collected Poems,* p. 524.
[13] *The Sacred Canopy: Elements of a Sociological Theory of Religion* (Garden City, N. Y.: Doubleday & Co., 1967), p. 33.

one who is himself the answer? Do we seek to overcome fragmentation because we belong to a larger whole which is our true home? Does the event of wholeness attained indicate that the reality which ultimately supports us is itself holistic? Our total experience is rendered most intelligible if these queries are answered affirmatively.

Both the urge to seek integrity and the consciousness of realizing it point beyond themselves to an integrative process at the heart of reality which is best regarded as the activity of God—though he may often remain incognito. In terms of Christian faith, quest and fulfillment alike result from the presence of him who is "God and Father of us all, who is above all and through all and in all," and who aims "to unite all things in him, things in heaven and things on earth" (Eph. 4:6; 1:10). Our human dissatisfaction with fragmentation and the deep need we feel for health and wholeness spring from the creative and redemptive work of him whose goal for human life is a community of righteousness and love. Countless persons in their brokenness have experienced the healing which enables them to affirm with Whittier,

> We touch Him in life's throng and press,
> And we are whole again.

8 THE CALL TO RESPONSIBILITY

Human beings are most fully human in their realization of values. To be a person, whatever else it may mean, is to be capable of experiences such as those of beauty, truth, justice, love, community, work, and play which enrich life. Values like these enhance one another, but in their deepest meaning they are intrinsically worthful, desirable for their own sake. These are the "times of inherent excellence" celebrated by Wallace Stevens, the "peak experiences" described by Abraham Maslow. Though capacity for them and accessibility to them vary widely, to some degree they are open to all human beings.

Our experiences of value constitute one of our major intimations of transcendence. In them we confront much more than appears on the surface, a dimension of existence which cannot be adequately probed by rigidly scientific ways of knowing, something ultimate in human life which we do not produce but find. As Huston Smith suggests, reality seems to include "surprising corridors of worth that elude ordinary eyes." [1] Following these corridors perceptively, we may find ourselves encompassed by an activity which is the creative and nurturing source of the experi-

[1] Richardson and Cutler (eds.), *Transcendence,* p. 16.

ences we cherish most. It is therefore not surprising that thinkers who differ widely in other respects have agreed in making value central in their interpretations of religion and the meaning of God. In a classical definition Harald Höffding regards religion as "faith in the conservation of values," while Henry Nelson Wieman conceives God primarily as "the source of human good." Michael Novak puts the same emphasis in contemporary language when he writes: "God is experienced . . . as a life within which our lives draw nourishment for the operations we most value. He is the source of the values that move us, and of our movement toward those values." [2]

Moreover, the actualization of value presents itself to us not merely as a possibility or an opportunity, but as a responsibility. The life of value is not something taken for granted or even accepted with gratitude. It is experienced rather as an imperative. As real as our experiences of intrinsic worth is the awareness of our obligation to realize and extend them. We feel constrained to share in the creation and furtherance of the kinds of experience which we prize most. Indeed, this consciousness often confronts us with the urgency of an unconditional demand, a call to pursue the good which takes precedence over all else, even physical life itself.

Though "the good" here means the worthy or the truly valuable, and is intended to cover the whole range of value experience, the notion of an unconditional demand calls special attention to moral choices and actions. The imperative, "I ought to seek the best," connotes, "It is right (at least for me) to seek the best, and if I refuse I incur guilt." Thus the call to realize the maximum value has itself an ethical quality, and it comes to expression most noticeably in connection with the moral values. As we explore its

[2] Joseph Whelan (ed.), *The God Experience; Essays in Hope* (New York: Newman Press, 1971), p. 19.

religious implications, it should therefore be clarifying to lay particular stress on ethical responsibility.

This responsibility is both personal and social. On the individual plane Jean-Paul Sartre, though an avowed atheist, stresses man's human sense of accountability for what he may become, and acknowledges an inescapable mandate to use his own freedom responsibly. Yet the responsibility of the individual for his own life thrusts outward to become also responsibility for other persons, since his existence is conditioned by theirs, and since nothing can be good for one which is not good for all.[3] Other ethicists are at least as emphatic as Sartre in interpreting responsibility in social as well as individual terms. The imperatives of conscience call on us not only to speak the truth and develop our talents, but to love our neighbor, to promote justice, and to advance peace among the nations.

It is highly doubtful whether accountability can be understood in all its empirical richness apart from its reference to a more-than-human context. Many thoughtful persons report a sense of being grasped, claimed, or entrusted from some source other than themselves. Thus Gerhard Ebeling can write, "It is the mystery of human personal being that it is summoned from elsewhere, that it exists in response and as response, and that man is therefore wholly himself when he is not caught up in himself, but has the real ground of his life outside himself."[4] Responsibility is rooted in response, and the reality responded to has a dimension of depth which points beyond the purely human. The imperatives we have noted, as they operate in sensitive persons, claim a deeper sanction than mere tradition, custom, or social approval. They come instead with the force of something ultimate, and those who fulfill them are conscious of participating in some reality greater

[3] Above, pp. 99-100.
[4] *The Nature of Faith,* tr. Ronald Gregor Smith (Philadelphia: Muhlenberg Press, 1961), p. 115.

than themselves and surpassing human society. This consciousness gives rise to the judgment that our experiences of accountability and ethical obligation are best understood as resultants of the activity of God, though they are not always identified as such. Considerable support for this thesis can be found in both literature and contemporary life.

God in Human Response to Need: The New Testament

In the biblical writings a corollary of the divine demand for righteousness is the frequently recurring declaration that God is actively involved wherever justice is done and action is undertaken to meet human needs. Four passages in the Gospels provide vivid illustrations of this theme.

In the early Christian hymn in which Mary magnifies the Lord (Luke 1:46-55), centrally important in the list of occasions for rejoicing *in God* are events which, attributed to divine action, reverse the economic and political positions of the exploiters and the exploited: the discomfiture of those who cherish exaggerated notions of their own importance and disdain others; the overthrow of the strong from power and their replacement by those formerly impotent; the feeding of the hungry and the liquidation of the prosperity of the wealthy. The passage might consistently become the basis for an imperative: "If you really want to magnify the Lord, don't stop with words. Act now to remove the injustices of your society. Oust those who wield power for their own benefit, and give ordinary people the opportunities they deserve. Take away the unearned privileges of the rich, and provide the poor with the food, clothing, housing, and education which they need. When you do these things God will be there with you."

Similar injunctions are both implicit and explicit in the passage describing the preaching of John the Baptist. For Luke he is the great forerunner envisaged by Isaiah who calls on Israel to prepare for the Lord by making his paths straight:

> Every valley shall be filled,
> and every mountain and hill shall be brought low,
> and the crooked shall be made straight,
> and the rough ways shall be made smooth;
> and all flesh shall see the salvation of God.
>
> (Luke 3:4-6; Isa. 40:3-5.)

These words have been so often idealized and romanticized that we easily miss the announcement of the same kind of reversal and equalization which are found in the Magnificat. The baptism preached by John was one of "repentance for the forgiveness of sins," but the repentance demanded involved turning away from mundane attitudes like the racial and nationalistic arrogance which boasted, "We have Abraham as our father"; and the promised salvation of God was to be fullness of life for "all flesh." When John was asked what fruits would "befit repentance," he listed three examples: Those whose economic needs are met are told to share food and clothing with those who lack these necessities. Tax collectors are ordered to practice honesty and fairness. Soldiers are commanded not to take unfair advantage of those subject to their authority (Luke 3:10-14). If it is actions like these by which we make way for the coming of the Lord, it seems obvious that in them he himself is present.

The same message is unmistakable in Jesus' sermon in the synagogue at Nazareth, where he uses the words of Isa. 61:1-2 to declare his consciousness of being indwelt by "the Spirit of the Lord" (Luke 4:16-30). The signs of his divine commission are of one piece with those related to Mary's rejoicing and the preaching of John the Baptist:

> . . . He has anointed me to preach good news to the poor.
> He has sent me to proclaim release to the captives
> and recovering of sight to the blind,
> to set at liberty those who are oppressed,
> to proclaim the acceptable year of the Lord.

Significantly, when Jesus goes on to interpret his coming as fulfilling the words of Isaiah, he adds two historical references which enrage his hearers. During a great famine, he declares, Elijah ministered to a widow of Sidon in preference to the many Hebrew widows. Later, Elisha cleansed the leprosy of Naaman the Syrian, but did not cure any of the many lepers in Israel. These references to prophetic solicitude for foreigners make clear Jesus' own concern to lift his fellow countrymen above their narrow nationalism and racism. But they so infuriated his audience that they tried to lynch him by throwing him off a cliff.

The broader implications of Jesus' conception of his commission and the aftermath of his statement of it should be clear. Wherever measures are undertaken to end poverty, to free men and women and children from the forces which hold them in bondage, to heal their physical infirmities, and to liberate the victims of oppression and exploitation, there God is actively present. And wherever efforts are made to actualize the oneness of humanity, there the one God of all nations is at work. These are ends sought by God himself. Inevitably, therefore, wherever and whenever human beings work in concrete ways for similar goals he is in their midst, and they are helping to advance his purposes whether or not they are aware of the full significance of their efforts.

This message is powerfully expressed in Jesus' portrayal of the Last Judgment in Matthew 25:31-46. The passage conveys three main emphases: (1) Only those who minister concretely to human need in its most earthly forms—hunger and thirst, lack of clothing, sickness, loneliness, imprisonment—inherit the kingdom of God. (2) Those who perform this practical ministry are actually serving God, since one of the forms in which the Eternal appears in temporal events—in Barlach's language, one of the "transformations of God" [5]—is in the likeness of people who sorely need the

[5] See above, pp. 80-83.

loving concern of others able to help. (3) Those who thus serve God in caring for their fellow human beings are unaware of the real meaning of their acts; they do not recognize the presence of God even though they could not be closer to him: "When was it that we saw you hungry and fed you?"

Two further implications of the parable deserve mention. First, it is a vivid reminder that the two "great" commandments which Jesus took from Deuteronomy 6:4-5 and Leviticus 19:18 and juxtaposed are at heart but two aspects of one imperative. When we love our fellows we love God, for he is in their midst; and our love for God is only a sham unless we love those whom God loves. Secondly, the passage offers an important corrective to the Christian exclusivism which is derived from statements like the declaration of Peter concerning Jesus Christ, "There is no other name under heaven given among men by which we must be saved" (Acts 4:12). In Matthew 25 "all the nations" are gathered before the King, who in separating the sheep from the goats asks nothing about the orthodoxy of their intellectual beliefs, but only whether they care enough about God's children to heal their hurts and thus to incarnate in life the faith they profess. When we take the New Testament in its totality, we discover that the "name" by which we are made whole is not only a word in our mouths but a Spirit in our lives. For Christians he manifests himself supremely in Jesus Christ. But the portrait of that manifestation in the Gospels makes plain that the test of our response is the genuineness of our self-forgetful love for other persons, especially the least and the lost. We show our ultimate trust in the God disclosed in Christ less when we give him a correct title than when we commit ourselves to the values he cherishes, whether we verbally relate them to him or not. "Not every one who says to me, 'Lord, Lord,' shall enter the kingdom of heaven, but he who does the will of my Father" (Matt. 7:21).

God in Human Response to Need: Later Literature

The theme which we have found so prominent in the Gospels appears frequently also in later literature. Dag Hammarskjöld comments on "the old fairy tale" in which "the one who has been made invisible can only regain his human shape through somebody else's love." [6] Just as old and widespread are legends describing the appearance of God in the acts of persons who minister self-forgetfully to suffering human beings.

In *The Little Flowers of St. Francis of Assisi* there is a moving story of Francis' meeting with a leper on the Umbrian plain. "Impelled by some power that had overcome his fear," Francis kissed the man whose disease aroused universal loathing, winning thereby the joyous and affectionate response of the leper. He then remounted his horse and rode off. According to the legend which soon grew up, Francis suddenly turned around, "but there was no one to be seen on the road at all. Then he knew that he had kissed the Lord." [7]

Closer to Matthew 25 is Tolstoy's story, "Where Love Is, There God Is Also," in which Martyn Avdyéich, a shoemaker, receives in a dream the assurance that the Lord will come to him the next day. Successively he provides tea and warmth for a man weakened by age and winter cold, food and clothing for a poverty-stricken young woman and her child, and understanding and reconciliation for a woman selling apples and a boy who tried to steal from her. At nightfall, as Martyn starts to read the Gospel, he seems to see in the dark corner of his room the figures of those he has helped, and three times he hears a voice saying, "It is I." His initial nonrecognition turns to joy as he reads the "inasmuch"

[6] *Markings,* tr. Leif Sjöberg and W. H. Auden (New York: Alfred A. Knopf, 1965), p. 115.

[7] Alan Paton, *Instrument of Thy Peace* (New York: The Seabury Press, 1968), p. 52.

135

of Matthew's narrative. Then he understands "that his dream did not deceive him; that the Saviour really called upon him that day, and that he really received him." [8]

"He who would see the Divinity must see Him in His children." So writes William Blake, whose poetry frequently returns to this theme, treating it with extraordinary simplicity and vividness:

> He doth give His joy to all:
> He becomes an Infant small,
> He becomes a Man of Woe,
> He doth feel the sorrow too.

For Blake, God's presence in things human becomes most manifest in the attitudes and actions which express ethical concern for people as people, regardless of race, nationality, or religion. This is true because God himself, whatever else he may be, is the ultimate ground or locus of the highest human values.

> To Mercy, Pity, Peace, and Love
> All pray in their distress;
> And to these virtues of delight
> Return their thankfulness.
>
> For Mercy, Pity, Peace, and Love
> Is God, our Father dear,
> And Mercy, Pity, Peace, and Love
> Is man, His child and care.
>
> For Mercy has a human heart,
> Pity a human face,
> And Love, the human form divine,
> And Peace, the human dress.
>
> Then every man, of every clime,
> That prays in his distress,

[8] Edward Wagenknecht (ed.), *The Story of Jesus in the World's Literature* (New York: Creative Age Press, 1946), pp. 421-27.

Prays to the human form divine,
Love, Mercy, Pity, Peace.

And all must love the human form,
In heathen, Turk, or Jew;
Where Mercy, Love, and Pity dwell
There God is dwelling too.[9]

Ignazio Silone's *Bread and Wine* is a powerful statement of the same insight, though with a realistic recognition that he who practices seriously the virtues extolled by Blake often confronts bitter opposition and grave danger. From start to finish the novel implies that God himself is active, though under a pseudonym, in Pietro Spina's selfless, nonconformist struggle for a new society, with the odds so overwhelmingly against him in Mussolini's Fascist Italy. In one tense passage the author comments on Pietro's action in writing an anti-war slogan on the wall of a public building:

If one poor man gets up in the middle of the night and writes on the walls of the village with a piece of charcoal or varnish, "Down with the War," the presence of God is undoubtedly behind that man. How can one not recognize the divine light in his scorn of danger and in his love for the so-called enemies?

The central motif of the book appears also in the story of Luigi Morica, a poor youth who for a time is a student in the faculty of letters in Rome. Because of his peasant background he is ridiculed and rejected by the other students. He then joins a revolutionary group, mainly because of their acceptance of him. Arrested, he becomes under the pressure of economic necessity an informer for the police. He is deeply in love with a girl in the group, but leaves her in anger when he misunderstands as disloyalty her consent to sexual relations with two policemen to save him from arrest.

Burdened with a sense of his guilt and in inner turmoil, Luigi

[9] Morrison, James Dalton (ed.), *Masterpieces of Religious Verse* (New York: Harper & Brothers, 1948), pp. 84, 139-40; see also p. 464.

finds peace when he confesses to Don Benedetto, an aged priest, and "Don Paolo Spada," the revolutionary Pietro Spina who has evaded the Fascist authorities by disguising himself as a priest. However, he goes to Don Benedetto "not because he was a priest but because in my eyes he has always been the symbol of the just man." He also cautions Don Paolo, "I didn't come here for pardon, or for absolution." This elicits from Don Paolo the admission that he is not really a priest, but the fugitive Pietro Spina. Thus the cleansing, renewing action of God occurs through two men, one a real priest sought out as simply a just man, the other a lover of human freedom whose priestly role is discharged only under a pseudonym.[10] God too, Silone is saying, performs much of his work incognito, in the courageous efforts of human beings who at whatever personal risk throw themselves into the struggle for justice and peace.

It would be easy to dismiss these ideas as merely the well-meant but unwarranted romanticizing of poets and tellers of tales. To do so, however, might accord less with the way things really are than to accept them as true. A firm basis for this conclusion may indeed be found in the very structure of reality as we experience it.

In a remarkable passage William Ernest Hocking calls attention to the common world which relates human beings to one another and enables them to communicate. He notes first the wall which seems to separate human beings, compelling them as it were to look at one another from behind impenetrable masks. Reflecting on his relation to a comrade, he imagines what it would be like if his mind could somehow be within the mind of the other, so that there would be no barrier between them. Then he suddenly realizes that such a relationship actually exists. Imagining himself addressing the other, he writes:

[10] *Bread and Wine,* pp. 275-76, 281-95.

But I *am* in thy soul. These things around me are in thy experience. They are thy own; when I touch them and move them I change *thee*. When I look on them I see what thou seest; when I listen, I hear what thou hearest, I am in the great Room of thy soul; and I experience thy very experience. For *where art thou?* Not there, behind those eyes, within that head, in the darkness, fraternizing with chemical processes. Of these, in my own case, I know nothing, and will know nothing; for my existence is spent not behind my Wall, but in front of it. I am there, where I have treasures. And there art thou, also. This world in which I live, is the world of thy soul: and being within that, I am within thee. I can imagine no contact more real or thrilling than this: that we should meet and share identity, not through ineffable inner depths (alone), but here through the foregrounds of common experience; and that thou shouldst be—not behind that mask—but *here,* pressing with all thy consciousness upon me, *containing* me, and these things of mine. This is reality.[11]

One does not have to share Hocking's apparent epistemological monism to perceive the significance of his recognition of the common basis of our discrete human experiences of nature and values. There is persuasive logic also in his conclusion that the underlying connectedness which makes persons potentially a community, not a chance collection of solitary individuals, is the very presence of God. Our capacity for knowledge of, and fellowship with, other finite persons is rooted in our common relation to an Other in whom we are united. "It is through the knowledge of God that I am able to know men; not first through the knowledge of men that I am able to know or imagine God." [12] Moreover, the light shed by the theistic reference on our knowledge of other persons extends equally to other aspects of our interpersonal relations, including our responsibility for contributing where we can to the fullest realization of their personhood. It is in God that we

[11] *The Meaning of God in Human Experience* (New Haven: Yale University Press, 1912), pp. 265-66.

[12] *Ibid.,* pp. 197-98.

can meet, know, and care for one another. When we evidence concern for our fellow human beings we are dependent on, even moved by, the divine reality which binds us together. By the same token, we are manifesting the divine Presence—whatever name may be given to the manifestation by those involved.

God in Human Response to Need: Contemporary Life

When we act in love to free other persons from their impediments and to enlarge their opportunities for worthy living, we are both drawing upon and disclosing the transcendent ground of our life together. That is to say, our actions have a sacramental quality; the divine Presence is mediated not only by the bread and wine of the Lord's Supper, but by the whole of our earthly existence when it becomes the locus of mutually supportive relationships. In the words of Nikos A. Nissiotis, *diakonia* is "the Eucharist *incognito,* represented in another way." [13] Illustrations of this broadened representation of the divine reality are by no means confined to the biblical writings or other literature. They abound in the day-by-day lives of men, women, and children in the world today.

One member of the graduating class of Wesley Theological Seminary in 1973 was David Seah Doe of Monrovia, Liberia, who was seeking further equipment for the ministry which he had already begun in his native land. For economic reasons he had been forced to leave his wife and two children in Africa. The boy, Kike-Nyandeh, had a severe impairment in hearing caused by an attack of measles when he was three. Incapable of distinguishing sounds clearly, he was also unable to learn to talk normally—a handicap which steadily became worse. There was some hope that surgery might correct the defect, but no one with

[13] "The Ecclesiological Significance of Inter-Church Diakonia," *The Ecumenical Review,* 13(1960-61), 193.

the specialized skill was available in Liberia, and a journey to a medical center offering the necessary facilities seemed out of the question.

Late in the spring of 1972 Professor Dewey M. Beegle and several students at Wesley Seminary, deeply concerned about the increasingly dark prospect confronting the lad, then aged ten, resolved to do their utmost to make possible the needed medical attention. An otologist was found who offered free surgery if an operation proved desirable. The major obstacle was the cost of transportation, a problem complicated by the fact that Irene Doe would have to accompany her son and also bring Tarnyonnor, the four-year-old daughter who could not be left alone. A total of over $2200 was needed—seemingly an impossible amount. However, articles were placed in the *Wesley Journal,* a weekly publication of the seminary community, stating the facts and appealing for financial help. Many individuals contributed, and some student pastors found a ready response in the churches they served. One of them, Lynn Buttorf, began by raising $271. Another, Randall Pratt, secured gifts totalling $770, including $500 from the Rotary Club in Ellicott City, Maryland—a demonstration of both their sensitivity to a concrete human need and the esteem in which they held this young minister. By the end of October the needed funds were in hand, plane tickets were purchased, and the family arrived in this country on the day after Thanksgiving.

A serious problem arose immediately when housing arrangements previously made proved not to be feasible. However, the United Methodist charge at Chewsville, Maryland, was completing a new parsonage, and offered the older house for the Does, though it would not be vacated until two weeks later. This problem was surmounted when the family of Paul Doherty, student pastor at nearby Smithsburg, offered to share their home during the interim. In the meantime, the congregations secured gifts of furniture, food, and money and purchased winter clothing for the family, so that by mid-December the Does were happily settled in their new community, surrounded by the affection of rural people who had never before had a black family in the neighborhood.

Thorough examinations of Nyandeh's hearing were conducted by Gallaudet College in Washington, several ear surgeons, and the Maryland State School for the Deaf in Frederick. These disclosed that the defect was neural, hence not subject to correction by surgery. His only hope lay in a good hearing aid and training in a school for the deaf. Further tests determined which of the fifty-odd types of hearing aids was best suited to his needs. The gifts previously contributed, totalling $2630, proved sufficient to cover the $368 needed for ear molds and the intricate hearing aid.

The Maryland State School has excellent educational facilities for the deaf, but state law limits their use to residents. This proved to be no serious difficulty. Though John Schildt, pastor of the Chewsville Church, and his wife had three daughters, including an adopted Indian child from Arizona, they decided it would be fitting to have a boy in the family. Hence John assumed the responsibility of becoming Nyandeh's legal guardian, and the lad became a boarding student at the State School. In June, following David's graduation from Wesley Seminary, he and his wife and daughter returned to Liberia. Nyandeh is now receiving systematic speech therapy and training in communication, along with a general education, and spending weekends and holidays with his American family. Since English is the major language of Liberia, he will be equipped for effective life and service in his homeland.

A long and difficult process lies ahead, but the situation has changed radically, and the outlook is highly promising. Because a boy and his family were surrounded by the loving care of other human beings who acted on their concern, he is being released from the prison of his stunted, closed-in existence, with the prospect of achieving healthy personal development in normal relations with other persons.

The practical regard for others which reached across an ocean to care for the Doe family is an almost literal embodiment of Matthew 25:35-36: "I was a stranger and you welcomed me, . . . I was sick and you visited me." Somewhat less personal are many movements that illustrate the more revolutionary thrust of the Lucan passages cited earlier in this chapter, and which command wide participation. Such movements call for changes in society which sometimes go to the roots of the social structure. Even professing Christians seem less likely to discern the hand of God in them than in deeds that minister directly to the needs of individuals and small groups or provide relief to sufferers from disaster. But there is no sound reason for such a distinction. Wherever conscientious men and women struggle for recognition of the dignity and rights of persons, for equality in education, housing, and employment, or for peace among nations, in response to an inner imperative which they cannot ignore, the God who is exalted in justice is actively involved. Possibly he is moved to act in unexpected ways, incognito, precisely because so many of his worshipers seek to confine him, for their private advantage, to support of the status quo.

Millions of Americans were outraged by their country's military involvement in Indochina in supposed fulfillment of promises to the aristocratic dictatorship which wielded power in South Vietnam. Opposition was aroused particularly by the unprecedented extent of the bombing which often destroyed nonmilitary targets like schools and hospitals; the defoliation of vast forests; the devastation of thousands of acres of rice paddies essential to the food supply of friendly as well as hostile Vietnamese; the burning of innumerable villages and hamlets; the killing of helpless civilians on an unprecedented scale by the use of weapons like napalm and anti-personnel bombs which caused maximum suffering; the creation of several million homeless people; and the apparent un-willingness of the United States government to listen seriously to the anguished protests of many of its most concerned citizens.

Their consciences aroused by such events, large numbers of people, representing all ages and educational levels and varied ethnic, social, and economic backgrounds, joined in a succession of peace marches, sit-ins, teach-ins, and other demonstrations, almost entirely nonviolent, in all parts of the country. People of deep religious convictions joined humanists and atheists in efforts to bring the killing to an end. All alike were caught up in devotion to an enterprise greater than themselves which spoke to them with commanding authority. All found unity with other persons in a common cause, enrichment of their lives through commitment, sometimes sacrificial, to a goal transcending their private interests, and a sense of meaning through their response to a love which would not let them go.

Similar enthusiasms have been generated, notably in the nine-teen-sixties, by the struggle for civil rights of racial and ethnic minorities. Triggered by events as different as the Supreme Court decision in 1954 outlawing segregation in public education and the bus boycott in Montgomery, Alabama, led by Martin Luther King, Jr., a series of demonstrations called forth the participation of hundreds of thousands of people of all ages, black and white, Catholic, Protestant, Jew, and humanist, laity and clergy, male and female, united in their urgent demand for the just implementa-tion of the human rights asserted by the Constitution of the United States. The call for "Freedom Now" has been voiced not only by blacks, American Indians, and Chicanos affirming their own dignity and their rights as human beings, but by hosts of whites who have felt constrained to join in the struggle. This broad base of support was much in evidence nationally in the grape boycott led by Cesar Chavez, which resulted in the unionization of the California grape pickers.

Worldwide support has been aroused in opposition to policies of *apartheid* in South Africa and the denial of basic human rights to the black majority in Rhodesia. The ranks of the Africans and their white Christian supporters such as Alan Paton and Bishop Colin Winter (now administering his Namibian diocese from exile in London) have been augmented by other persons who basically as humanitarians have felt irresistibly the weight of the demand for justice. On the contrary, such movements have been hampered, especially in South Africa and Southwest Africa, by the readiness of some church bodies to accept without protest gross violations of basic human freedoms. This makes all the more significant the recent actions by various denominational agencies to end their tacit support of racism in Africa by withdrawing their investments in corporations which derive profit from exploitation of black labor and provide economic support for current repressive polities.

In movements like these in behalf of social, economic, and political justice many religious persons have experienced in dedicated action an awareness of the living reality of God which far surpasses in vividness and power anything which they have known as participants in corporate worship in church or temple. Others have found in such activities a fulfilling extension of congregational worship which was already rich in meaning. Thus the distinguished Jewish theologian Abraham Heschel remarked, "When I marched with Martin Luther King in Selma, Alabama, I felt my legs were praying." [14] Likewise, large numbers of persons who have not ordinarily regarded themselves as religious have found themselves gripped by a cause, a goal, or a spirit which has claimed their commitment with all the force of an ultimate concern. Though the reference is explicit in one case and implicit in the other, the experience seems to be essentially the same in

[14] *Newsweek,* January 8, 1973, p. 50.

both groups. It points to the presence of the God who at every level is "wrapped up" with the destinies of individuals and peoples.[15]

Prominently involved in both the antiwar movement and the struggle for human rights in America and other lands have been large numbers of students and other youth. The wide response to the appeal for Peace Corps volunteers and later to VISTA has been matched by the willingness of many students to give their time in the tutoring of disadvantaged ghetto children and similar enterprises. Thousands of young people in colleges and universities have joined in opposition to the draft, to defense-related research, to military recruitment on campus, to income derived from industries heavily involved in the prosecution of the war—to all expressions of a close connection between higher education and the military and industrial status quo. Many youth have been repelled by the shallow materialism of their elders, the primacy of the success motive in American culture, the power of wealthy individuals and corporations in the political process, and the denial of fundamental rights to minorities. Positively, they have sought to discover and realize authentic personal values and to attain a greater measure of social justice. So broad has been the commitment to concerns like these that Robert N. Bellah was able to testify in 1969—in an International Symposium on the Culture of Unbelief held at the Vatican—to "the multitude of religious enthusiasms sweeping the American campus today." [16] The adjective is justified. The values sought by the youth involved have been for them a matter of supreme concern. Their action in behalf of the dignity and fulfillment of persons has occurred in response to an inner imperative which has outweighed all considerations of

[15] A. Christie H. Rosa, *The Living God,* ed. Dow Kirkpatrick (Nashville: Abingdon Press, 1971), p. 125.
[16] *Beyond Belief,* p. 223.

personal advantage or pragmatic calculation. They have been "turned on" to transcendence.

It must be admitted that some of these movements have been accompanied by excesses—as has often been true of traditional religion. It also seems clear that within the past several years much of the enthusiasm has waned. Disappointed and disillusioned by failure, public indifference, and the power of the established order to maintain itself, many have yielded to the attitude which says in effect, "What's the use?" However, this change in mood and the accompanying decrease in action do not cancel the historical reality of what has taken place, nor do they nullify the concrete results that give every evidence of being lasting. Civil rights have been granted a firm status in federal and state laws. Segregation in public accommodations has been abolished. Unprecedented numbers of black people are now exercising their right to vote; and many are winning election to important political offices previously denied them. The Rules of the National Democratic Convention have been decisively modified. The welfare of ethnic and racial minorities is on the consciences of increasing numbers of Americans. The peace movement which originally represented only a small minority eventually aroused majority support for ending the war in Indochina.

It would also be erroneous to regard diminished enthusiasm as invalidating belief in a transcendent dimension in the commitments described. An ebbing tide does not destroy the actuality of the flow which preceded it. Many religious movements have come and gone in human history, often with long-range effects, and the questions of their ultimate significance and whether or not they were the work of God can never be decided purely on the basis of their longevity. Actually, the decline in fervor among the young may say more about the limitations of human beings than about the reality of God. It speaks volumes concerning the unwillingness to change of millions of adults who have profited from the status quo, and the apathy of other millions who prefer the relative security of the present order to the uncertainties of new proposals. It also reflects a lack of experience, realism, depth, and perspective on the part of many of the youth themselves as they have confronted the inertia and hostility of the established order. Such developments are not the first occasion where human shortcomings have hampered fulfillment of the purposes of God.

Few aspects of American life are more depressing than our treatment of criminals and delinquents and our attempt to deal with civil disorder by forcible repression without attention to causes. With relatively few exceptions our prisons incarnate a philosophy of retributive punishment which functions to bring out the worst in both guards and inmates. Our "correctional" institutions are often schools of crime rather than instruments of rehabilitation. In them persons are more likely to be dehumanized than prepared for playing a constructive role in society. In this brutalizing atmosphere bloody riots like the one at Attica, New York, in 1971 become practically inevitable. To all this the public responds with large-scale indifference and demands for violent suppression. In spite of overwhelming evidence of volcanic unrest in our prisons and failure in our systems of criminal justice, most people remain indifferent, content to place offenders behind walls and forget them.

Yet even in this dark picture there are some bright spots. Enlightened persons are heeding the biblical imperative to "proclaim release to the captives"; yet the deliverance they seek is not only from physical confinement, but from the personal, interpersonal, and environmental factors which constrict life and lead to antisocial behavior. The use of wisely supervised probation instead of incarceration is winning increased acceptance. Paroles administered with understanding and alertness to individual needs are producing encouraging results. Halfway houses are equipping growing numbers of persons for the acceptance of full freedom and responsibility. Groups of concerned persons like the one based in First Community Church, Columbus, are organizing events inside and outside the Ohio State Penitentiary in which honor-dorm prisoners participate with members of the congregation. They are also seeking to improve guard-prisoner relationships and carrying on community education and corrections research. The Prison Release Ministry of the United Methodist Northern Illinois Conference is helping prison inmates to maintain contact with society outside—and thus to counter debilitating isolation—through letters and visits from people who care. Promising youths in considerable numbers are now preparing for careers in criminal justice. Comparable sensitivity is combined with mature wisdom and wide experience in the extraordinary Report of the National Advisory Commission on Civil Disorders,[17] occasioned by the violence which erupted in many parts of the United States in 1966 and 1967. Though composed of "moderates," the commission headed by Governor Otto Kerner of Illinois really listened to the voices of the ghetto and produced a document that in both its analyses and its prescriptions should command the active support of both concerned citizens and governmental agencies. As Tom Wicker has written, it is "a report on America—one nation, divided," and "we are not likely to get a better view of socially directed violence —what underlies it, what sets it off, how it runs its course, what follows." [18] By many it has already been relegated to the back shelves, but some are taking it seriously and seeking to give effect to its realistic and far-sighted recommendations.

Insight and intelligent concern regarding the treatment of offenders and the conditions which produce them are by no means limited to persons who are themselves safely removed from prisons and from the areas where riots usually occur. When desperate

[17] Introduction to *Report of the National Advisory Commission on Civil Disorders* (New York: Bantam Books, 1968), pp. ix, xi.
[18] *Ibid.*

inmates demanding complete release took over Cellblock I of the one-hundred-year-old District of Columbia jail in October, 1972, and held eleven guards hostages for twenty-four hours, some of the most constructive action came from prisoners. Kenneth L. Hardy, D.C. Corrections Department Director, at great risk voluntarily entered the cellblock to talk with the rebel leaders, becoming himself a hostage. Concerned citizens such as Representative Shirley Chisholm of New York, D.C. Delegate Walter Fauntroy, D.C. school board president Marion Barry, Petey Green, head of Efforts from Ex-Convicts, and attorneys Julian Tepper and Ronald Goldfarb, listened and negotiated. The U.S. District Court held an extraordinary session which heard grievances and changed the atmosphere from one of armed confrontation to one of consideration of positive remedies. But also highly significant were two developments from the side of the prisoners. The majority of inmates are not serving sentences, but awaiting trail, and many of them wait as long as eighteen months to go to court. The jail population includes juveniles, since by law youths sixteen or older are tried as adults if charged with murder, rape, or other serious felonies. One of the pleas of the prisoners was that "the kids" sixteen to eighteen years old be placed in a separate section away from older inmates with criminal records. "Give them a chance for a decent life," was the appeal, "before it's too late." Important influence was exerted also by William G. Brown, a ringleader in the rebellion, who was able to convince his companions that the court hearing had achieved concrete results and that the hostages should be released. At least partly because of his calm counsel, the lives of the hostages were spared and a bloody dénouement was averted. Four days later Brown was sentenced to five to twenty years on the robbery charge for which he had been jailed.

Such incidents demonstrate eloquently the right of offenders to be treated as persons rather than animals. They also manifest the movement of the Spirit of God. In them the Word is becoming flesh anew and dwelling among us. In them can be heard the voice of one who says, "I am there in all the walled and unwalled prisons which confine people today and obstruct their freedom. Anything you do to bring release to the least of these my brothers advances my own liberating work." In such events God himself is acting—incognito, but with transforming power.

While we are examining contemporary instances of responsible commitment to high human values in fulfillment of a supreme concern, we cannot soundly omit the past quarter-century in the People's Republic of China. Though the country is officially atheistic, Chairman Mao's call, "Serve the people!" has elicited in his followers an enthusiastic dedication to the welfare of all. The health and total well-being of each individual is the concern of the whole people, and vice versa. Visitors remark on the religious quality of the commitment of workers at all levels to the goals of the new China. Amazing results have been attained in a short span of time in an economy still largely dependent on hard manual labor. There is no unemployment. Famines and food shortages are absent. The average family has decreased in size from eleven or twelve members to three or four. Food and population are in balance. The people are healthy, with medical care available to all. The aged are provided for. Illiteracy has been ended. There is neither venereal disease nor prostitution. The country has finally won admission to the United Nations, and is pursuing peaceful relations with other nations near and far.

It has been observed that the ethical norms of China today constitute in effect a socialized version of puritanism. More significantly, the social policies which have liberated hundreds of millions of people from prisons of poverty, hunger, sickness, and ignorance are carrying out on a scale unprecedented in human history the kinds of action interpreted in Matthew 25 as service to God. Ironically, all this has been going on while many professing Christians in the West, blinded by emotional hostility to "godless" communism, have seen in such movements in China and elsewhere only a deadly enemy to be opposed at all costs. Unquestionably, Communist governments have sought, often aggressively, to suppress religion. But when we inquire why, the answer is often linked in part to the passivity of churches and Christians in the presence of social evil and the frequent identification of Christianity with the injustices of the status quo.

God in Human Irresponsibility

In Jesus' parable of the sheep and the goats God is declared to be present in people needing help even when those able to minister to them fail to respond. Persons guilty of such irresponsibility evoke the stern word of judgment: "The curse is upon you. . . . Anything you did not do for one of these, however humble, you did not do for me" (Matt. 25:41, 45 NEB). This negative side of the parable is a vivid reminder that women and men encounter God not only when they seek justice and mercy in human relations, but equally when they willfully or indifferently ignore the claims of their fellows. The accusations of the unheeded conscience may point as genuinely to the divine reality as do acts of deep social concern.

Peter Berger states this truth with shocking vividness when he includes among present-day "signals of transcendence" the conviction of many sensitive people that inhumanity is not merely despicable, but damnable—worthy of ultimate reprobation. Less jarringly, but with equal perceptivity, William Temple asserts that our sense of failure to do our duty may be the voice of God, since it presupposes the presence in human life of that which calls us to concern for others and sensitivity to the claims of high values.[19]

[19] *Nature, Man, and God*, pp. 334-35.

Recent history affords illustrations enough of debilitating feelings of guilt, not only in individuals but in large segments of American society. Those who lived through the period of the assassinations of John and Robert Kennedy and Martin Luther King, Jr., cannot easily forget the agonizing soul-searching which these events elicited in all parts of the nation. "What has gone wrong with our country?" people asked again and again. "What has happened that we can spawn such violent disregard of all that we cherish most? Where have we lost our way?" On a smaller scale, events like the riots in Watts and Attica aroused the consciences of myriads of people to realize the vastness of the chasm between the equal opportunity we profess to believe in and the oppressive ghetto existence to which we condemn so many of our fellow citizens. But probably nothing in our national experience can approach the alienation and guilt produced in millions of Americans by their complicity, however indirect, in the death and destruction wrought by their country in Vietnam, climaxed by the final fury of the bombing of Hanoi and Haiphong.

Such events provide outstanding instances of the gap between what we are and what we feel we ought to be. Our consciousness of this hiatus points to an implicit awareness of God. The knowledge of our unholiness, writes Hocking, "is already a touch of the untouchable and a beginning of holiness." It is the underlying relation to God which

reveals to man the disparity between himself and his world, sets him at odds with that from which he came, brings him to that pass to which the animal cannot come—an unwillingness to take his world as he finds it, a consciousness of the everlasting No, and a defiance of it or perhaps a subservience to it—as if *this* were his god. And what man has to learn by degrees is, that it is his original knowledge of God that has made this alienation possible.[20]

[20] *The Meaning of God in Human Experience,* pp. 238-39.

All human beings know the temptation to make ultimate some partial, finite element in their experience, to treat patently limited claims as unconditional. This temptation is nowhere more apparent than in the demand to place the partial interests of individuals or groups above those of society as a whole. When we recognize our conditional, fragmentary values for what they are and accept the obligation to rise above them, we are responding to the presence within us of a norm, a claim which demands that we judge our actions by their relation to the whole to which we belong. This recognition is a sign of the judgment of God, and it is the beginning of our salvation.

Here it becomes clear again that the effective presence of God does not depend on the conscious recognition of that presence by human beings. There are persons who either verbally deny any transcendent reality or live without conscious reference to it, but who in fact acknowledge the unacceptability of their own limited commitments and the evil of unjust social policies, and feel summoned to correct both. By their attitudes and actions such persons implicitly ascribe trans-subjective validity to the norms by which they feel judged. By contrast, there are professed theists who belie their profession by their idolatrous attachment to ends which thwart the attainment of authentic human values. In both cases God is active as the Critic of the self-centered pretensions and false ultimates which alienate human beings from one another and from him. He who sometimes acts pseudonymously to summon women and men to responsible action also operates incognito as Judge of their irresponsibility.

God and Conservative Movements

Most of our contemporary illustrations of the presence of God in responsible human action have dealt with efforts to alter some existing situation. Noting this, some readers may well ask, Is not

God concerned with preserving the good in the present order? On what basis do you identify him with liberal, even radical, causes but not with conservative action? Why mention marches organized by groups like the Southern Christian Leadership Conference but omit the Daughters of the American Revolution? Why cite Martin Luther King, Jr., but not Billy Graham, who does not take public stands on social issues? Why applaud the antiwar activities of the Berrigans, while leaving out Carl McIntyre's demonstration at the Washington Monument demanding military victory, and support of the war by Cardinal Spellman, who in a Christmas sermon in South Vietnam in 1966 told the men in the U.S. armed forces that they were "soldiers of Christ"? Have I simply chosen men and movements I like and arbitrarily given them the blessing of God? These are fair questions, and they make plain the need to explicate the criteria which have been operating.

I make no claim to freedom from subjectivity, and no doubt personal preferences and biases have played their part. The perspectives of a lifetime cannot be easily set aside. However, I have sought to apply as objectively as possible guidelines that would be accepted as valid by people of differing social orientations.

Throughout this chapter I have been guided by the three-fold conviction that human life is distinguished chiefly by the capacity to realize values; that our value experience is grounded in something ultimate which exercises normative authority; and that this dimension is best understood as the activity of God, who seeks among women and men the maximum fulfillment of value. Hence the imperative to actualize and extend experiences of intrinsic worth is an expression of the life of God in our midst, though his presence often remains unrecognized. Obedience to this imperative may entail sometimes support of existing social arrangements, at other times effort to change them. But whether either policy is to be regarded as fulfilling the purposes of God depends on its probable contribution to the advancement of human values. Since the values sought by the God of all mankind are universally human, we are prohibited from identifying him with movements aimed at securing advantages for any nation, race, or class at the expense of others. But many present social practices are of this restrictive kind, calling forth vigorous action to universalize opportunities for the fullest enrichment of human life. In such movements we can rightly affirm the presence of God.

Closely related to these considerations is the conception of God stated in the Preface and assumed throughout these chapters. If he is Being at the heart of all existence, he provides the stable, dependable order which is necessary if life is to be possible. But this order is not static, mechanical, or cyclical; it must be related to the other aspects of the life of God as we have conceived him. If he is personal Love, he is actively identified with attempts to heal the rifts which divide individuals and groups; and with efforts to further relationships of mutual trust, cooperation, and justice. If he is dynamic Process, he is himself involved in the creation of the new, and we can rightly look for him in human endeavors to discard outmoded institutions and to open the way to enlarged opportunities for the enrichment of life. Hence our understanding of God, though it was arrived at on other bases, commits us to take change seriously.

For those readers whose Christian faith commitment, like my own, leads them to seek ethical guidelines in the biblical writings, it is appropriate to summarize here the norms that are implicit in the New Testament passages cited earlier in this chapter. These are in harmony, I believe, with the ethics of the New Testament as a whole and with the teachings of the great Hebrew prophets. They have exerted profound influence on my own thinking. According to these sources, attitudes or actions like the following may be taken as manifesting the active presence of God.

1. Awareness of human need and serious commitment to meeting it in love, in response to an experienced inner imperative.

2. Concern for justice, liberation of people from oppression and injustice, and establishment of conditions necessary for abundant life.

3. Extension of this concern to all persons and groups, regardless of race, color, nationality, sex, or economic or social status.

4. Support for changes, radical though they may be, needed for the achievement of these ends.

5. The presence in society of signs of judgment on injustice and exploitation.

To a considerable degree my discussion of the presence of God in contemporary responses to human need has been guided by norms like these derived from my understanding of the New Testatment revelation. There is of course room for different interpretations, but all professing Christians must take serious account of the teachings prompted by the momentous events connected with the coming of Jesus Christ. These events should tell us something crucial about the ways in which God is working in the world today.

It is my belief that the New Testament criteria should commend themselves to non-Christian humanitarians also, even as the norms based on the experience of value are worthy of acceptance by Christians. Indeed, each approach may find something approximating confirmation in the essential concurrence of its findings with those of the other. Whether we begin with the New Testament portrayal of the locus of divine action or with the manifestation of God in the imperative to realize maximum value, we come out at the same place.

9 THE PULL OF THE NOT-YET

A basic characteristic of human existence is its orientation toward the future. This may appear in various forms: the awareness of something lacking which elicits effort to supply the lack, pressure toward fulfillment of "the not-yet," the urge to realize possibilities so far unattained and only vaguely intuited. Human beings are pilgrims on the way, drawn toward an unknown future, and sustained by hope that their aspirations may be attained. In this dimension of our experience we may find another intimation of transcendence. Though it has been noted in passing in earlier chapters,[1] it is worthy of special consideration.

Recognition of this forward thrust of human life is found frequently in the interpretations of sociologists, psychologists, and philosophers who are not seeking to defend a theological position. Thus Robert Bellah believes that the unsatisfied longings that are so characteristic of our existence often bear witness to the genuine need for change in the existing situation, and can therefore be taken to convey truth regarding the structure of reality.[2] Peter

[1] See above, pp. 30-31, 69-70, 102-3, 113-14, 124.
[2] *Beyond Belief,* pp. 198-99.

Berger lists as one "signal of transcendence" the hope with which men and women habitually face the future, even when they are threatened by defeat and death. Man's "no!" to death, both his own and that of others, sometimes expressed in death-defying acts of self-sacrifice, "appears to be an intrinsic constituent of his being," reflecting a life-affirming hope at the core of his *humanitas.* Though "empirical reason" may indicate that the hope is illusory, such hope and the courage it engenders are also empirically grounded, growing out of "those implications or intentions within experience that transcend it." [3]

Karl Jaspers sees human beings as involved in "the Encompassing," which denotes both what they themselves are and Being itself, in and through which they are. The Encompassing which we are has three modes: our empirical existence, consciousness as such, and spirit. As spirit, it is the temporal process which finds fulfillment amid constant change. "Out of a continuously actual and continuously fragmenting whole, it pushes forward, creating again and again out of its contemporary origins its own possible reality." Since spirit is oriented toward the whole, it relates everything to everything else, but in an active movement in which the present "is never finished yet always fulfilled."

The Encompassing that we are is integrally related to the Encompassing that is Being. This has two modes: the World of empirical existence, which can be investigated by universally valid procedures; and Being itself, or Transcendence. But the reason which discloses the relation is neither a "timeless permanence" nor "a quiet realm of truth." Though it seeks unity, it is "the binding, recollecting, and progressive power whose contents are always derived from its own limits and which passes beyond every one of those limits, expressing perpetual dissatisfaction." For Jaspers there is no rest but always movement in temporal existence.

[3] *A Rumor of Angels,* pp. 75-81.

This action issues forth "from the ultimate substantial ground-movement in the tension between the individual and the universal, between the actual and the total range of the possible, between the unquestionable immediacy of existential faith and the infinite movement of reason." [4]

Another contemporary form of the conception of human life as pointed toward the future in active hope is found in the thought of liberal European Marxists. Julius Tomin of the Charles University in Prague has put it simply: "Man should endeavor to realize the optimum of his life." [5] At the meeting of the *Paulus-Gesellschaft* in Salzburg in 1965, Marxists no less than Christians recognized "the prospective character of human existence," though for Christians the "transcendence" implied in this datum provided an answer, while for Marxists it took rather the form of a question. According to Roger Garaudy, Marxism accepts the empirical reality of what Christianity has called a consciousness of "the superhuman in man" or man's capacity for the infinite. But instead of referring this to God, Marxists transpose it into men's awareness of their incompleteness, their consciousness of their as yet unrealized possibilities, which they are summoned to fulfill in their concrete earthly situation. [6]

This stress on the open-ended movement of human life is prominent in the philosophy of Ernst Bloch. In Bloch, however, it is grounded in a carefully constructed metaphysics. His thought is therefore peculiarly relevant in the present context.

When rightly seen, declares Bloch, New Year's Eve and New Year's Day interpenetrate; epilogue and introduction run together. The real is a multiple process which links the present with the

[4] "The Encompassing," *Problems and Perspectives in the Philosophy of Religion,* ed. George I. Mavrodes and Stuart C. Hackett (Boston: Allyn & Bacon, 1967), pp. 422-28, 430-34.

[5] Conversation in Prague, November 26, 1966.

[6] *Christentum und Marxismus—heute,* ed. Erich Kellner, p. 77.

uncompleted past and above all the possible but undetermined future. "Man stands again and again out in front on boundaries which are such no longer: in perceiving them he passes beyond them." [7] Bloch uses three main categories to express his dynamic view of reality: front, the new, and matter.

1. Both human existence and the world as a whole are marked by movement along a constantly changing front. In every now we are moved by our awareness of, or hunger for, something which is *not-yet,* but which through our effort may become real. This sense of not-having is future-oriented; it is informed from ahead by the having for which it hopes. Truly understood, therefore, "Genesis is not at the beginning but at the end." Adapting the language of formal logic, Bloch puts his message with utmost brevity in the formula, "S is not yet P." Subject is not yet predicate. No subject has at any given time the predicate that is adequate to it. Everything is under way. The history of being itself is its experimental attempt to identify itself and its origin. Its real essence is nothing fixed that is already there, but rather latency for something, tendency toward something. Thus human beings are participants in a risky expedition whose point of departure they cannot imagine, but in which they are called to transcend every present. Their supreme good is the kingdom of freedom symbolized by the biblical images of the Exodus and the kingdom of God. But they must seek its realization without guarantee of success from any already completed transcendent reality. [8]

2. The basic distinguishing quality of the whither of reality is

[7] *Tübinger Einleitung in die Philosophie,* I, 8; *Das Prinzip Hoffnung,* pp. 225, 284-85.

[8] *Philosophische Grundfragen,* pp. 7-9, 18, 25, 39; *Dokumente der Paulus-Gesellschaft,* ed. Erich Kellner, XII, 118-19; *Tübinger Einleitung in die Philosophie,* I, 177; *Das Prinzip Hoffnung,* pp. 17-18, 1566, 1625-26, 1629.

found in the *novum*. Resulting again and again from the dangerous pilgrimage of men and nature toward the not-yet is the emergence of genuine novelty. The process is not a gradual unfolding of something already present in a kind of capsule or chrysalis, but a leap into the new. Instead of leading to the realization of some foreordained purpose, as in the old teleology, it brings forth real *nova*. The future must therefore be taken with complete seriousness; it is never merely repetition of the past or the working out of what was already there in germ. Purposes form themselves in the active process of life, arise ever anew, and never reach finality.

Since the world process is ultimately mysterious and cannot be precisely known, it is best described in parables and symbols. Bloch employs a variety of metaphors, some of them biblical, to portray the new. Without apology he uses the term *Utopia* (literally *no place*) to express the direction of the movement of reality toward events which have never yet occurred but which are really possible. In world literature this notion is formulated in terms of non-alienation, freedom, happiness, the golden age, the eternal feminine, and the trumpet signal in *Fidelio*. Bloch frequently refers to it as the homeland, meaning not whence we have come, our place of origin, but our true destination, where we really belong, which is on the way toward ever-new fulfillments.

Here one thinks naturally of the gods of time in Greek mythology, such as Eos, Nike, and Hermes. Bloch finds them rightly portrayed as having wings; nevertheless, they are far less adequate than the "Time-God" Jahweh when he, full of the future, defines his name to Moses as "I will be what I will be" (Exod. 3:14). Understanding is vastly enriched when we rise above the succession of *chronos* or clock time to the *kairos* or "filled" time of John the Baptist or Thomas Münzer, which "originates" in itself, and in which new events happen. In such suggestions we find the deepest meaning of images like Exodus, the Promised Land, the coming kingdom, and the new heaven and the new earth; and of affirmations like "I am the resurrection and the life," and "Behold, I make all things new." [9]

3. The clue to both the not-yet and the new is to be found in matter, which for Bloch is the ultimately real. Matter, however, is no changeless stuff or passive substance, but constant activity. It "ferments" in all our experiences of lack, and fulfills itself above all in forward striving. Authentic materialism is dialectical, synthesizing the truths of both idealism and materialism. Matter must therefore be conceived dynamically and qualitatively, as the ultimate ground of a world of process and hope. As suggested by its cognate *mater,* it is the source of all real possibilities, the fruitful womb from which are born man's future and its own. It is the substratum of both the movement and the novelty of existence; from its creativity arise both the phenomena of subhuman nature and all the values sought in human society. The already real is surrounded by a limitless sea of potentiality, out of which novel, unforeseen, and unfixed forms of reality may emerge. In all this there is no such thing as a pre-existent, finished transcendence, a secure castle to which travelers turn for succor and guaranteed security. Instead there is "a transcending without heavenly transcendence," the possibility which outruns and exceeds every past attainment, the "grace" (*sic*) which enables man to be "wanderer and compass and land together at the front."

Bloch's philosophy of hope is a this-worldly eschatology in which human beings themselves play an indispensable role. They are the wanderers, and they must chart their own course into the unknown. Their hope is one in which they "have not only something to drink, but also something to cook"! That is, they have work to do which will not get done unless they do it. Bloch puts this graphically by declaring that matter needs its

[9] *Das Prinzip Hoffnung,* pp. 17-18, 1625-27; *Dokumente der Paulus-Gesellschaft,* ed. Erich Kellner, XII, 113, 118-19; *Tübinger Einleitung in die Philosophie,* I, 176, 185.

boldest figure of organic life and organization, Promethean man, if all the salutary processes of the future are to be set in motion and fire is to be kindled on the earth. Men and women confront on their way decisive alternatives both threatening and promising, and the choices which can translate possibilities into realties are theirs alone. As they make them, however, they can rely on the total world process which provides the necessary objective basis for the realization of the possible. The revolutionary change which for Bloch is implied by all these motifs—the not-yet of the front, the new, and matter—occurs thus through the joint activity of socialized man and nature. Free people working in an open environment, cosmic as well as social, are the secret of an effective journey toward our homeland. The human subject actively hopes in a cosmos which makes hope hopeable.[10]

All the thinkers just surveyed find in human existence an activity which pulls men and women toward the future realization of hitherto unexplored possibilities. Powerfully active in our lives are promptings, hopes, and aspirations which outrun all previous accomplishments and draw those who experience them toward new fulfillments. Some interpreters are willing to use the name *God* for this transcendent dimension, though they prefer less traditional language. Others emphatically reject both the name and the ideas associated with it, since God for them means a timeless, changeless, static Absolute whose preconceived and predetermined ends allow no real initiative or freedom for human beings.

Without question the history of Christian doctrine discloses many instances of belief in a static deity, with Aristotle's Unmoved Mover playing a decisive role. God has sometimes been

[10] *Das Prinzip Hoffnung,* pp. 287-88, 333-34, 1522, 1627, 1629; *Philosophische Grundfragen,* pp. 31-32; *Dokumente der Paulus-Gesellschaft,* ed. Erich Kellner, XII, 114-15, 117; *Geist der Utopie* (Frankfurt am Main: Suhrkamp Verlag, [1918] 1964), p. 347; *Tübinger Einleitung in die Philosophie,* II, 178-79.

portrayed as somehow comprising past, present, and future in an eternal now of perfect fulfillment. Under the influence of theologians of the stature of Augustine and Thomas Aquinas the end of history has been conceived as the felicity of eternal repose in the heavenly city or the perfect vision of the divine essence in a timeless eternity.[11] Thinkers like Bloch, finding this conception sharply at variance with the empirical reality which they encounter, regard atheistic naturalism as a sounder interpretation. However, in drawing this conclusion they overlook the possibility of another understanding of God that would take full account of the data which they rightly regard as important.

As Bloch himself recognizes, the God who leads his people toward a new future is proclaimed again and again in the biblical writings. It is true that the Bible repeatedly affirms the permanence of God, the contrast between the transitoriness of created things and the eternity of the Creator, "the Father of lights," in whom "there is no variation or shadow due to change" (James 1:17; Ps. 102:26-27; cf. Mal. 3:6; Heb. 13:8). However, such passages do not assert a stationary perfection; they are concerned rather with emphasizing the utter dependability of God, who is not subject to the perishability and evanescence which mark finite things. He can always be counted on, and his steadfast love endures forever. But those who worship him are told to expect the unexpected and face the future with hope for new creations.

In faith and hope Abraham answers the command to migrate to an unknown land (Gen. 12:1-3; Rom. 4:13, 19). The history of his descendants is that of a covenant people on the way in response to the promise of God who is himself en route. He discloses himself to Moses as "I will be who I will be," or "I will do what I will do" (Exod. 3:14). He covenants with Israel to

---

[11] Augustine, *The City of God,* X, 14; XIX, 17; XX, 30; Thomas Aquinas, *Summa Contra Gentiles,* XLVIII, LI.

lead them out of bondage in Egypt into a new land, going before them in a pillar of cloud by day and a pillar of fire by night (Exod. 13:21-22). Centuries later, in a new situation with new needs, he makes a new covenant, written not on stone but in the hearts of his people (Jer. 31:31-34). He acts to "put a new spirit within them" (Ezek. 11:19). He assures his followers, "When you pass through the waters, I will be with you. . . . I will bring . . . , I will gather . . . , I will say . . ." (Isa. 43:2, 5, 6). He arouses in his people hope for the coming of the Messiah and a kingdom of righteousness which will have no end (Isa. 2:2-4; 9:1-7; 11:1-9; 32:1-8, 15-18, 20), and he acts to "create new heavens and a new earth" (Isa. 65:17).

Significantly, the Christian gospel is first made known in the life, teachings, death, and resurrection of one who had no place to lay his head, and was with his disciples more often on a dusty road or in a boat headed for a new destination than in the safety of the harbor. The resurrection itself looks forward rather than backward, pointing toward the future in hope. "He is not here," says the "young man" to the women at the empty tomb. "He is going before you" (Mark 16:6, 7)—an assurance which provides for Moltmann and others major grounding for their theology of hope. In the Gospels as in the other New Testament writings a constantly recurring expectation is that of the coming of the kingdom of God. The early Christians are typically referred to in the New Testament as people of "the way." The God revealed to them in Jesus Christ is "the God of hope," who "gives life to the dead and calls into existence the things that do not exist" (Rom. 15:13; 4:17). For the author of Hebrews faith is "the assurance of things hoped for," and it is based on the promise of him who is faithful. We do not yet see all things subject to the rule of God, "but we see Jesus," the pioneer of salvation. Hence we are called to move out in hope to "seek the city which is to come," on the way considering "how to stir up one another to love and good works" (Heb. 2:8-9; 10:23-24; 11:1; 13:14). Similarly, the author of II Peter urges his readers to await and *hasten* the coming of the day of God, who has promised "new heavens and a new earth in which righteousness dwells" (II Peter 3:12-13). The element of newness is stressed also in the Apocalypse, which envisages the coming of the new Jerusalem, "a new heaven and a new earth," through the deeds of the God who makes all things new (Rev. 3:12; 21:1, 5). The falsity of the view which interprets such eschatological passages in purely otherworldly terms is shown equally by the prominence of the ethical note and the fact that the promised kingdom includes earth no less than heaven.

A survey of the history of Christian thought concerning God would show that, in spite of a strong absolutistic tradition, biblical teachings like the above have sometimes exerted weighty influence. However, such a survey does not belong to our present concern. It is sufficient to point out that in the twentieth century the God who is understood by many theologians to call forth men's faith, worship, and service bears notable resemblance to the cosmic activity which Bloch finds laboring to produce the new and summoning human beings to join the struggle. Here one thinks readily of the *élan vital* in Bergson's creative evolution, of Whitehead's God in process, and of Teilhard de Chardin's omega principle. In one letter Teilhard expresses his desire to abandon himself actively to "the presence and action of God. To be in communion with Becoming has become the formula of my whole life." [12] Elsewhere he describes his thought as "a neo-humanism that looks to the future." [13] Similarly influenced by evolutionary thought, Edgar S. Brightman finds in our human experience of God not only

[12] To Claude Aragonnès, May 19, 1941, *Letters from a Traveller* (New York: Harper & Brothers, 1962).
[13] Letter to George B. Barbour, October 2, 1948, in Barbour, *With Teilhard de Chardin in the Field* (New York: Herder and Herder, 1965).

"eternal purpose" but also "creative novelties." We are led by the very nature of the creative imagination and the purposive character of personality, both human and divine, to recognize that the goals of God include "new creations." [14] The Christian humanist Nikos Kazantzakis portrays this forward thrust in mythical language. "Blowing through heaven and earth, and in our hearts and the heart of every living thing, is a gigantic breath —a great Cry—which we call God." The successive forms of life, such as plants, worms, and eventually men, are content to remain undisturbed as they are; they resist change. But the Cry is merciless: "I am beyond. Let go of the earth, walk! Leave the mud! Stand up!" Human beings are centaurs, with equine hoofs planted in the earth but with bodies from breast to head urged on by the Cry. This is "the evocative, purposive love" of God, which "calls the generations from the beginning" (Isa. 41:4), summoning men to leave present securities and satisfactions and venture toward the fulfillment of their true destiny as children of God.[15]

The eschatological implications of Paul Tillich's view of God as the ground of being are not always recognized. However, they appear clearly in the third volume of his *Systematic Theology* when he discusses the kingdom of God and "essentialization" as the goal of history, and they are unmistakable in *The Shaking of the Foundations.* Here he makes clear that the depth or ground of history which he identifies with God is nothing inert or fixed. It is rather "infinite and inexhaustible." It is both source and aim of our life in society and of what claims our unreserved commitment in ethical and political action. "Perhaps you should call this depth 'hope,' simply hope." When the prophets of Israel were enabled to look beneath the appearances of their times to deeper

---

[14] *A Philosophy of Religion* (New York: Prentice-Hall, 1940), p. 385.
[15] *Report to Greco* (New York: Simon & Schuster, 1965), pp. 291-92.

levels they discovered hope. In our era too the activity in the depths of reality calls us to move forward in expectation.[16]

Within the past decade various Christian theologians, sometimes influenced in part by Bloch, have laid special stress on hope and the future in their thought of God. Thus for Jürgen Moltmann the coming God, promising a new world of truth and righteousness, calls the currently real into question because it is not yet what it can become. " 'History' arises in the light of its end," and its driving force is the promise of God.[17] Johannes B. Metz recognizes the importance of unfulfilled human expectations, but finds them pointing beyond the human. God calls men and women to participate freely and actively in possibilities which are not merely a projection of human qualities, but rooted in the nature of God himself.[18] Karl Rahner speaks of God as "the absolute future"— the ultimate ground of our projection or planning of a future. The wholeness of man's future can never be expressed in this-worldly terms alone. The transcendent condition of human possibility is God.[19] Similarly, Wolfhart Pannenberg understands God as "the Power of the Future." The transcendence of God is to be conceived not "as a lifeless beyondness, but as a living, ever new carrying out of his freedom, and thus as the making possible of future, life, new event in the world." [20]

The foregoing survey discloses among thinkers who differ widely in many respects a basic consensus on the presence in human

[16] *The Shaking of the Foundations* (New York: Charles Scribner's Sons, 1948), p. 59.

[17] *Theology of Hope,* pp. 164-65, 260-61.

[18] *Christentum und Marxismus—heute,* ed. Erich Kellner, pp. 109-10.

[19] *Ibid.,* pp. 221-28; "Gott vor uns," *Ernst Bloch zu ehren,* ed. Siegfried Unseld (Frankfurt am Main: Suhrkamp Verlag, 1965), p. 232.

[20] "Der Gott der Hoffnung," *Ernst Bloch zu ehren,* ed. Siegfried Unseld, pp. 217-19; *Theology as History,* ed. James M. Robinson and John B. Cobb, Jr. (New York: Harper & Row, 1967), p. 250.

existence of a dynamic thrust toward a future which we are summoned to seek in hope. Humanistic naturalists and Hebrew-Christian theists agree that history is not simply the automatic unrolling of what is already contained in the past, but that it brings forth real *kairoi,* creative moments which exhibit genuine novelty, and which involve more than the exertion of observable human powers.

This view, moreover, is not mere pious romanticism. The new actually does occur, giving human beings opportunities to face the future with openness and creativity. Obviously reality is such that this is possible. Human striving takes place in relation to an activity which transcends it, pulling it onward toward the actualization of unforeseen possibilities. We confront, then, the question of how best to interpret this activity.

All in all, the view which grounds human hope in the activity of God offers the most coherent account of the experienced data. The major emphases of Ernst Bloch, for example, make more sense if interpreted theistically. Indeed, he reads into the term *matter* wider and deeper meaning than it can support without drastic redefinition. The qualities which he ascribes to it transform it into something more akin to consciousness or spirit, or at least to a synthesis of spirit and what matter has historically connoted. The word is not sufficiently rich and many-sided to describe accurately or adequately the reality which he regards as ultimate. More light is shed on the powers and activities which he finds at work in the world process if they are grounded in the creative, energizing actuality of the personal life who in love interpenetrates all existence and ever seeks to realize maximum value.

The truth of this judgment may appear more clearly if we look briefly at several specific terms which frequently recur in Bloch's exposition of his philosophy of hope. Hope itself implies someone who hopes; it can hardly apply to the universe as a whole unless it denotes something more than an unknowing movement or force.

The concept of novelty presupposes a mind that can compare and relate the freshly emergent with what has preceded it, even as the notion of a not-yet presupposes some reality that, aware of time, can with memory of the past and consciousness of the flowing present anticipate the future. The purpose which "intends" the actualization of potential values and draws finite persons to participate in the process implies the functioning of something akin to conscious intelligence. Though "grace" may refer symbolically to those factors in our total environment that help us on our journey, it gains its full meaning only as an unearned gift bestowed by a Giver who consciously imparts his transforming power and forgiving love. Moreover, the biblical motifs embraced by Bloch are inseparable from the biblical faith in God which he rejects: the Exodus occurs under the guiding providence of God; the promised land requires a Promiser; the kingdom is the rule of God; the hope that does not disappoint is based on the love of God; it is God who brings the new. Bloch removes these themes from their theistic foundations and attributes them to an artificially reconstrued matter. It would be more in accord with their central intent, and with the experiences which they reflect, to incorporate them in a dynamic concept of God that relates him closely to the movement, struggle, and hope of the world we know.

There are therefore strong grounds for ascribing the pull of the future in human experience to the living God of transforming love who awakens and strengthens us and sets us on the way as workers with him. Christian eschatology yields nothing to Marxism or other non-Christian views in its concrete concern for the well-being of people in earthly history. The long-range goals of the God of the future are normative now; they call for the removal of injustice and the extension to all persons of unhampered opportunity for fullness of life. Christian faith likewise affirms emphatically the responsibility of human beings to participate actively in the realization of future possibilities. However, all their efforts occur in response to the creative, redemptive, and liberating activity of God, who leads them toward the new creation and empowers them to share freely in its coming. They may not fully recognize what is happening, but when they heed the demand to seek a better future they may truly be said to experience the effective presence of the divine.

PART

3

THE COGNITIVE VALUE OF
RELIGIOUS EXPERIENCE

10 THE REALITY OF GOD

"After reading W. James, I still want to know if my religious experience is an experience of God or an experience of myself."—Étienne Gilson[1]

In the foregoing chapters we have surveyed not only occurrences regarded by those who report them as personal encounters with God, but also a broad range of experiences which point toward the presence of some reality that transcends the human. We have asserted that some experiences of both types may be best understood as experiences of God, who in the second type of event is presumed to be present incognito. At various points (e.g., pp. 93-94, 100, 109-13, 130-31, 138-40, 170-72) we have dealt with critical questions as they have arisen. However, until now we have undertaken no systematic evaluation of the basic position advanced. Such scrutiny cannot be avoided. The whole inquiry would be of dubious value, to say the least, if it did not seriously weigh the soundness of its central thesis. We therefore need to examine the truth of the claim of the experiences

[1] *Reason and Revelation in the Middle Ages* (New York: Charles Scribner's Sons, 1938), p. 97.

dealt with to bring those who have them into relation with a divine presence whose reality is prior to, and independent of, that relationship.

The claim to experience something implies that what is experienced has some kind of objective reality. The signification of statements like "I was radiantly happy" or "I felt deeply disappointed" is quite different from that of assertions such as "I saw a Canada goose" or "He heard the fire siren." Feelings of joy and regret may occur without a definite objective referent, but geese and sirens exist whether we experience them or not. Statements in this volume about experiences of the transcendent purport to be of the latter kind. They imply that *experience* refers not merely to a psychological state, but to a reality whose existence is independent of its being encountered. We have now to ask whether this belief in an objective reference is justified.

We have found much evidence that women and men are open to the transcendent, and that many of them think they are confronted by it. The question remains, Is the transcendent actual? Are the experiences noted simply projections of ourselves, or are they authentic experiences of God conceived as the dynamic, personal love which is the ultimate ground of all being and becoming? Do they yield cognitive truth regarding the existence and nature of the transcendent reality presumably encountered?

At the start it should clear the air if three admissions can be made. (1) Any answer to this question, affirmative or negative, will be colored by subjective factors. The personal interests and feelings of the thinker inevitably affect the weighting he gives to different aspects of the evidence and hence the conclusions reached. (2) There is no way of proving or demonstrating beyond all possibility of doubt the reality or unreality of the object of our cognitive efforts. Nothing approximating the precision of the natural sciences is open to us in this area of inquiry. (3) It follows that no universal agreement can be expected. Differences in psychological makeup, environmental factors, and varying perspectives insure that differing answers will be given to the same questions by thinkers searching for truth with equal sincerity. Nevertheless, the inquiry must be undertaken, and it can be hoped that the judgment reached will command respect even from persons who do not concur.

Religious Experience: Claims and Problems

There is a givenness about religious experience which demands that it be taken seriously. Persons who have experiences which they consciously identify as religious think of themselves as encountering an objective world, and many feel themselves to be in the presence of the transcendent source of all reality. Typically, faith in God is not arrived at as the result of a step-by-step process of logical reasoning. Instead, the believer simply finds himself interpreting his experience in this way. Nor is religious experience of this kind ordinarily treated as a rational basis from which one argues his way to theistic belief. For example, James W. Jones writes that the experience of Jonathan Edwards "was not a warrant for faith (defined as assent) but was the very *fact* of faith (defined as a new perception). His certitude was akin to the certitude of the givenness of experience and not that of a good deduction." [2] Though the believer's awareness of God often falls short of the assurance and intensity characteristic of Edwards, it is important, and usually fundamental, in his total grasp of reality. Such experiences are sufficiently widespread that they cannot be summarily dismissed as erroneous or insignificant. The same may be said of those broader perceptions of transcendent reality which are not consciously referred to a divine presence.

[2] "Reflections on the Problem of Religious Experience," *Philosophy of Religion and Theology: 1971,* ed. David Griffin (Chambersburg, Pa.: American Academy of Religion, 1971), p. 121.

If, however, we proceed on the assumption that such experiences yield dependable knowledge of a reality that is independent of human subjects, we immediately encounter problems. Three of these merit consideration here.

1. The given factuality of experiences of the transcendent is not in itself decisive evidence for the reality of the object to which they refer. Psychological assurance, even certainty, is no guarantee of cognitive validity. Neither subjective awareness of God nor experienced intimations of transcendence more broadly conceived are self-authenticating. Three considerations should suffice to make this clear.

a. Persons who report with equal confidence that they have "met" God often differ widely regarding the nature of the God presumably encountered. These differences sometimes amount to contradiction; the experiences described, however vivid, cannot refer to the same objective source. Religious experiences inevitably reflect the backgrounds, concerns, and hopes of those who have them. As Leibniz observed, everything expresses the universe from its point of view; hence what we say about God may tell much more about ourselves than about him!

b. Many thoughtful and honest persons report no experiences which they can attribute to divine activity. They remain therefore unconvinced by believers' accounts of experiences which to the latter are completely convincing. If religious experience in itself is to be accepted as decisive evidence of the independent reality of its presumed source, the absence of such experience must be given equal weight as evidence for nontheistic conclusions. Such an impasse cannot soundly be accepted. Instead, both positions must be critically examined as far as possible in relation to the total context of human experience and thought.

c. Religious experiences may be mistaken in their claim to involve a divine reality independent of the experient. The believer may declare that he is as conscious of God as he is of himself, but there is always the possibility that his inner awareness is erroneous. Many "realities" believed in because of vivid feelings have turned out to be illusory, and religious feelings are not exempt from this danger. The words of Thomas Hobbes remain pertinent for believers as well as for skeptics:

If any man pretend to me that God hath spoken to him . . . immediately, and I make doubt of it, I cannot easily perceive what argument he can produce to oblige me to believe it. . . . To say he hath spoken to him in a dream, is no more than to say that he dreamed that God spoke to him. . . . So that though God almighty can speak to a man by dreams, visions, voice, and inspiration; yet he obliges no man to believe he hath done so to him that pretends it; who (being a man) may err, and (which is more) may lie.[3]

Leaving Hobbes and his suggestion of deception aside, the possibility of error and self-deception is clear. There is no path that leads unerringly from psychological states to knowledge of the real world. Religious experience, like other forms of our human encounter with reality, must be critically examined with a view to ascertaining the truth of its objective reference. Both the believer and the unbeliever should profit by such scrutiny. Here it should be pointed out that a lack of religious awareness has in itself no greater cognitive validity than has an unexamined feeling awareness of God. The absence of religious experience cannot alone qualify as demonstration of the absence or unreality of the God affirmed by religious believers. Persons who do not report experiencing God may be just as subjective and open to error as those who claim a personal encounter. Both believers and unbelievers stand to gain, therefore, by an effort to examine the truth claims of religious faith.

    2. This inquiry cannot be pursued with the methods of precise

[3] *Leviathan,* Chap. 32.

measurement and tightly controlled experiment utilized by the natural sciences, where the main data are supplied through sense perception. The similarities are greater than are often recognized. Both approaches interpret data found in experience, and neither can prove beyond all possibility of doubt or later disproof that the object or objects it seeks to know are real independently of the minds conducting the investigation. Nevertheless, there are important differences between investigation of the physical world and study of religious experiences, and the methods appropriate to the former cannot without considerable modification be carried over to the latter. This inevitably leads to less definiteness and less agreement in the conclusions reached in religious inquiry than in the physical sciences. As John Hick has shown, sense perception has a certain coerciveness and a universality that are lacking in religious perception, and religious awareness varies with different individuals far more than does sense experience. Religious experience may also be compelling for those who have it, but apparently no one is required to have it, whereas sense experience cannot be avoided. The God witnessed to by religious believers uses persuasion rather than coercion. This characteristic of religious phenomena underlies the diversity noted, since it opens the way to degrees or levels of religious awareness, ranging all the way from absence of religious concern to intense God-consciousness.[4]

But such differences between the two approaches do not justify the judgment that sense perception is dependable while religious perception is not. Alfred J. Ayer begs the question when he claims that the argument for transcendent being is "altogether fallacious," since there is no way of verifying it "empirically." [5] He arbitrarily

[4] *Faith and the Philosophers* (New York: St. Martin's Press, 1964), pp. 242-47.

[5] *Language, Truth, and Logic* (New York: Dover Books, 1952), p. 119.

assumes that sense experience alone is empirical, providing our only road to truth. A more empirical procedure would recognize that experience is many-sided, so that no one method may be qualified to deal with all the data encountered. As objects of human cognition the physical world and the God of religious faith are very different, and it is only to be expected that different ways of knowing will be required. If God proves not to be discoverable by sense experience, the first response of the genuine truth-seeker will be not to deny his reality, but to ask whether another method of inquiry might yield different results.

Actually, there is no cause for wonder in the fact that the senses cannot find God—though there would be occasion for surprise if the opposite were true. If God is, he is not a constituent of the physical world, a finite thing among many other finite things, but the creative activity that underlies, interpenetrates, relates, and sustains them all. If, as suggested above, God is conceived as the dynamic personal love who is the ultimate ground of all being and becoming, he could not be apprehended by any of the senses or by all of them together. But he might be known in personal communion, thought, and sensitive participation in experiences like those we have tried to describe—depth, dependence, meaning, responsible action, and hope.

In this connection it is important to emphasize the significance, already mentioned, of the freedom of human beings to respond differently to events which themselves are susceptible of diverse interpretations. Even the sciences, involving as they do theoretical explanation as well as observation of experienced data, often fall short of the exactitude, certainty, and agreement frequently attributed to them. For example, the wave theory and the corpuscular theory of light account for the observed phenomena equally well; and modern physicists, instead of maintaining that either alone is true, tend to regard them as descriptions of complementary aspects of one reality [6]—though with no clear proof of this supposition. The possibility for divergent understandings is much greater in the realm of religious experience.

Thinkers as different from each other as Pascal and Whitehead agree in calling attention to the important role played in the interpretation of religious data by human attitudes not determined but freely chosen. Pascal maintains that God purposely orders his self-revelation so that he can be found by those who seek him while remaining hidden to those who do not. "There is enough light for those who only desire to see, and enough obscurity for those who have a contrary disposition." [7] Whitehead's God acts by "persuasion"; he exerts power by "the worship he inspires." He is "the poet of the world, tenderly leading it by his vision of truth, beauty, and goodness." [8] John Hick, taking his cue from Pascal, suggests that human beings can enter into a truly personal relationship with God only if they are moral agents capable of relatively independent choice. Hence God does not force on them a consciousness of his presence. He creates them with a tendency to interpret their total experience of the world religiously, but he does not compel this response; thus the tendency may be resisted or suppressed.[9] Seen in this light, religious experience and our interpretations of it exhibit the same variety which characterizes all our experiences of value. Added to the complexity and richness of the data is the fact that a truly personal and interpersonal life, capable of growth in the actualization of genuine worth, is impossible unless persons are free to make decisions of their own as to what is true and important and to respond accordingly to the reality they encounter.

3. A further problem appears in the position of some present-

[6] *Encyclopaedia Britannica* (1971), 13, 1128c.
[7] *Pensées,* No. 430.
[8] *Process and Reality,* p. 526.
[9] *Faith and the Philosophers,* pp. 247-48.

day interpreters who assign to religious experience important symbolic meaning while denying that it has any cognitive significance. In Robert Bellah's "symbolic realism," for example, symbols like God, Being, Life, and Nothingness serve to relate the manifold elements of our lives in a coherent whole of meaning, and in this way they are constitutive of persons and society, but they are noncognitive. They are unavoidable, but "fictional and provisional." Religious faith is "true" in the sense that it is intrinsic to the structure of human existence, but it is beyond both belief and unbelief, and yields no knowledge of anything objective. Referring to the religious enthusiasms characteristic of the American university campus several years ago, Bellah notes that they exhibited little concern over the conflict between science and religion which had previously been so vigorous. This attitude, he maintains, is traceable to the assumption that "religion is not a matter of objective cognitive assertion that might conflict with science, but a symbolic form within which one comes to terms with one's fate." "Religion is embodied truth, not known truth." [10]

A similar orientation is found among some logical empiricists and other linguistic philosophers, who are unwilling to follow the older logical positivism in treating theological propositions as meaningless or nonsensical because they cannot be empirically verified or falsified. Stimulated by the later Wittgenstein's recognition of multiple "language-games," these thinkers recognize that language may perform various functions. There is a plurality of languages, each with its own logic. Thus theological language may be in effect a recommendation of a way of life, with assertions about God seen as statements of ethical intention. It may in addition seek to evoke commitment on the part of other persons. It may be regarded chiefly as an expression of worship or aspiration. It may be primarily existential or personal, reflecting the individ-

[10] *Beyond Belief*, pp. 202-3, 221-22, 223. See above, pp. 66-67.

ual's consciousness of guilt, finitude, or mortality. It may give utterance to a fundamental attitude toward the world and recognition of the worth of this attitude for personal and social life. Or it may be seen as a kind of poetry, that may be not only aesthetically worthful but valuable in the formation of human character.[11]

However, most logical empiricists who now acknowledge meanings like these in religious experience and its appropriate language still deny to it any claim to referential truth. Partly because theological speech is not univocal but ambiguous, and partly because the objective reference of alleged experiences of God or the transcendent are not subject to sensory verification, these analysts regard such experiences as wholly noncognitive. Terms like *true* and *false* do not apply to them. Theological statements may be valid and meaningful expressions of human perspectives, attitudes, and volitional postures, but neither they nor the experiences which occasion them yield knowledge about any independent supersensible reality.

Though there are obvious merits in the above-mentioned views, their rejection of all cognitive significance in religious experiences is not convincing. In particular, three objections may be lodged against it.

a. It is highly doubtful whether the noncognitive functions of religious faith can be maintained if they are divorced from all epistemic reference to divine reality. Bellah is right in insisting that the enactment of faith is more important than logical demonstration or doctrinal correctness, but his dictum that religious truth is embodied, not known, is itself a half-truth.

[11] See the writings of D. M. MacKinnon, R. B. Braithwaite, R. M. Hare, John Wisdom, J. J. C. Smart, Willem Zuurdeeg, I. T. Ramsey, and Ian Crombie. Clarifying discussion of their views may be found in Frederick Ferré, *Language, Logic, and God* (New York: Harper & Brothers, 1961), Chaps. 10 and 11. See also John A. Hutchison, *Language and Faith* (Philadelphia: The Westminster Press, 1963), Chap. 4.

In support of it he declares that "the life of the church has been its capacity to produce human beings who base their lives on the paradigm of the Gospels, the saints and martyrs, even modest and hidden ones, who have constantly renewed it and are renewing it today." [12] He forgets, however, that Christians whose self-giving love has exerted renewing power have based their lives not on a paradigm, but on belief in the living reality of the God proclaimed by the Gospels.

The same oversight occurs in the proposals of various linguistic analysts to restrict religious language to certain noncognitive functions. Affirmations of faith in a righteous God or a transcendent ground of human responsibility do constitute a recommendation of a way of life, but this recommendation is inseparably connected with convictions about the nature of reality. The call to commitment springs from belief in the object of commitment. The attitudes of worship expressed in much religious language ordinarily imply faith that a real relationship is attainable between the worshiper and the object of his devotion. The concern here is not to claim that these beliefs must therefore be accepted as true, but simply to show that to exclude them from the functioning of attitudes which integrally involve them leaves us with some unfinished business. The language of faith purports to refer cognitively and truly to a real state of affairs. If this function is taken away human experience of the transcendent loses its distinctive quality, without which the other functions are called into serious question.

b. The denial of cognitive value to experiences of the transcendent because of the ambiguity of the language used to describe them depends on an unjustifiably restricted conception of the use of language. Wittgenstein's famous assertion that "what can be said at all can be clearly said" is far from

---

[12] *Beyond Belief*, p. 221.

self-evident—though his implied plea for maximum clarity must be heeded. It is true that the word *good* may be used to describe a dog, a food, a concert, or a person, obviously with different connotations, so that the sense in which it is applied to God requires refinement. But this is flimsy ground for excluding it from religious discourse. It is also true that religious people often vacillate in their use of terms like goodness, love, and purpose in relation to God, subjecting them to what Antony Flew has called "the death of a thousand qualifications." [13] This should goad theologians to seek utmost clarity and consistency in their conceptions, but it provides no adequate basis for the abandonment of their inquiry.

There is a wide agreement among thoughtful human beings that concern for the welfare of others is good, and that it may even entail willingness to give one's life for other people or a cause that aims to benefit them. The examples of Jesus, St. Francis, Mahatma Gandhi, and Martin Luther King, Jr., come readily to mind. There is no way of defining without any ambiguity a value like "concern for human welfare," but to exclude it from discourse because it lacks univocal meaning or precision would render thought incapable of dealing with aspects of human life which urgently require attention. The same is true with many of the terms and concepts used to characterize the religious life of humanity. The criterion of univocality is simply too neat and restrictive for the wealth and variety of the experiences that comprise life as we find it. In short, logical empiricism is not empirical enough for the data encountered.

c. The denial of cognitive meaning to experiences related to the transcendent because their objective reference cannot be confirmed by sense perception involves an arbitrary narrowing

---

[13] Flew, Antony, and Alasdair MacIntyre (eds.), *New Essays in Philosophical Theology* (New York: The Macmillan Co., 1955), p. 97.

of the field of significant experience. Flew maintains that statements about God or religious experience must be in principle verifiable or falsifiable by something that happens "in this world"—by which he means the physical order. If religious propositions cannot be confirmed or shown to be false on the same basis as nonreligious empirical factual statements, they are irrelevant to this kind of world.[14]

To this sweeping judgment the appropriate answer is, "Why?" On what basis other than the preference of the author can such an utterance be made? Why should we unquestioningly accept what is subject to examination by the senses as alone definitive of reality? It is fair enough to ask that religious assertions be judged by what happens in the world, but the world as it presents itself in day-to-day human experience is much broader and deeper than that known to the senses, and many things are happening there which demand other criteria of truth. In that world are I-Thou relations of friendship and love, appreciations of beauty, claims of conscience, and intimations of a presence calling forth ultimate concern. To rule these out as irrelevant to our human quest for dependable knowledge of the world because they do not fit a preconceived norm entails a drastic and unsupportable impoverishment of our existence. If the key prescribed does not fit all the doors of human experience, it is better to look for another key or keys than to maintain categorically that all doors but one have nothing behind them. Or to borrow an analogy from another critic, if we use a two-inch net and catch only fish longer than two inches, we are not entitled to assert that the sea contains no smaller fish, or that the possibility of their existence cannot even be discussed.

[14] Lecture by Antony Flew at American University, Washington, D.C., September 30, 1970.

Concern for maximum objectivity, undistorted by purely personal considerations, is necessary in strictly scientific investigation. It is a value to be respected also in other areas of our quest for knowledge and understanding, else we shall be at the mercy of private interests which will effectively bar the path to truth. But if complete objectivity is not to be had, the wise course is to use the methods of inquiry best adapted to the data being investigated. The question then confronting us is, What procedure should be followed when we are exploring the truth claims of our alleged experiences of transcendent reality? What should be our criteria? Further, when we apply them, what conclusions do we reach?

Religious Experience and Truth

Unless we are satisfied to treat religious experience as a special compartment separate from the rest of human life, the search for religious truth must be pursued in close relation to the quest for dependable knowledge in other areas.[15] In fact, best results are likely to be achieved if the procedure followed is broadly similar to that relied on by the sciences. The differences already discussed must be kept in mind, with particular attention to the relative comprehensiveness of investigation of claimed experiences of the transcendent and the impossibility of exact measurement in such inquiry. Four main steps are involved: the gathering of data found in historical and contemporary experience; the formulation of synoptic hypotheses suggested by the data; the testing and possible modification of the hypotheses in the widest possible context of human experience; and the drawing of conclusions most in accord with the evidence as a whole. In the examination of particular questions these stages are seldom so distinct or

[15] For a discussion of the grounds for this view, see my *God in an Age of Atheism,* pp. 139-47.

systematically followed as this listing would suggest, and often they are interwoven. Yet in some form they are all pertinent.

In the present context a fair sampling of the data may be found in the preceding chapters of this book. The "synoptic hypothesis" to be tested is the repeated affirmation that much personal awareness of the divine and many indications of a transcendent dimension in human life are best interpreted as the real presence of God. So to interpret our experience is not equivalent to using God to fill the gaps in our scientific knowledge of the world. It was this tendency to fall back on God to explain phenomena which are unexplained on known principles that in part accounts for Bonhoeffer's assertion that God "lets us live in the world without the working hypothesis of God." [16] The hypothesis here advanced is not that God is the cause of natural processes for which scientific explanations are lacking, but rather that certain experiences that point persons beyond themselves are most soundly understood in terms of the activity of God.

As used throughout this book the word God is taken to mean the dynamic personal Spirit who is the creative ground of all being and becoming and who in and through manifold interrelationships seeks the maximum fulfillment of value. Implicit in this statement is the conviction that God is best conceived as a unity of Being, Process, Love, and Personal Life, with no one of these conceptualizations—nor all of them together—able to express adequately the breadth and depth of his meaning. Thus the basic question before us is, Do experiences of the transcendent yield authentic knowledge of God so conceived and bring human beings into his presence?

Since the preceding chapters have already answered this double question tentatively in the affirmative, what is now called for is a critical evaluation of the answer. In this we shall be guided

---

[16] *Letters and Papers from Prison* (New York: The Macmillan Co., 3rd rev. ed., 1967), p. 196.

chiefly by four criteria: the internal consistency of the theistic interpretation; its harmonious relation to other human experiences and beliefs; its capacity to illuminate human existence and make it more intelligible; and its practical consequences. We need to ask: (1) Does the view that God himself is encountered in our experiences of the transcendent entail any inner contradiction? (2) Does it take account of historical religious experience and the broadest possible range of contemporary experience and thought, including knowledge gained from the scientific study of the physical order and the lives of persons in society? (3) Does it shed light on our experience as a whole, enlarging our understanding and deepening our sense of meaning? (4) Does the faith involved enrich life, releasing spiritual resources which enable persons to live with courage, hope, and loving concern for others?

Used in close relation with one another, these standards should provide helpful guidance. No norms, of course, can guarantee conclusions completely free of error. The data we seek to interpret are amazingly complex and pervaded with mystery. Moreover, subjective factors inevitably intrude on our best efforts to think objectively in religion, sometimes swaying the process unjustifiably toward conclusions that the thinker wants to reach. Thus equally serious investigators may emerge with widely different results. Hence the serious seeker for religious truth will offer every critical judgment with the implied addition, "So it seems to me," or, "From my perspective, this is how things look." Nevertheless, if the criteria suggested can be applied in this spirit, they should bring us as close to the truth as it is possible for finite minds to come.[17]

[17] The reader may note the omission of the Hebrew-Christian Scriptures from these criteria. As a Christian theologian I am constantly guided in my thinking and living by the biblical witness to God's creative and redemptive action in the world. This influence is apparent in the frequent references in the preceding chapters to biblical passages and events. However, it would be inappropriate to use a norm derived from my own faith

It seems wise not to attempt to evaluate here experiences involving a personal consciousness of God, like those discussed in Chapter 3. Such experiences vary widely, and would have to be examined individually—a long process not necessary to fulfill the purpose of this volume. Our central concern has been with experiences of the divine presence unrecognized as such by those who have them. In what follows we shall therefore concentrate on the intimations of transcendence considered in Chapters 4–9, with emphasis on the five main forms identified in Chapters 5–9. However, instead of examining each of these in turn, as before we shall let the criteria provide the structure.

In a review of the preceding chapters I can find no evidence of internal inconsistency in the judgment that God is active though often unidentified when persons experience depth, dependence, search for meaning and wholeness, responsibility for others, or the pull of the future. It could be readily shown, I believe, that there is nothing inherently contradictory in this proposition. We shall therefore concentrate attention on the other three criteria, in each case dealing with issues typical of those that arise when the possible theistic significance of these broad areas of human existence is considered.

1. *Is the theistic interpretation harmonious with the totality of human experience and of knowledge gained from secular sources?* The evidence as a whole supports an affirmative answer. The mystery, strangeness, awe, and wonder which often characterize

---

commitment as a criterion of evaluation for persons who do not share that commitment. When we are scrutinizing the soundness of affirming the presence of God in human experiences of self-transcendence, it would beg the question to turn for authoritative guidance to writings which proclaim the very truth we seek to examine! As indicated earlier (above, p. 60), we are attempting to do theology "from below," interpreting events found in ordinary human life as generally experienced. This suggests that our criteria also should be those likely to be recognized by anyone who is looking for truth concerning our human existence.

our existence—in scientific exploration of the natural order, artistic creation, and encounters with other persons—accord well with faith in the inexhaustible creativity of God. The intricate interdependence of human beings and the dependence of all of them for life and its values on a reality beyond or other than themselves makes sense if grounded in dynamic personal Love.

The claims of ethical and other values in human life are most understandable if they are perceived as rooted in the divine will. The imperative to responsible concern for others comes to us with the force of a claim, a summons, a call, suggesting that its source is a self-conscious Conserver and Advancer of values rather than a purely human sense of duty. This interpretation also harmonizes with religious experience. Historically, many sensitively religious persons have regarded God as active in concrete action to meet human need; and the impetus felt by many humanistic participants in movements for social justice is psychologically similar to that of religious believers involved in like movements.

The theistic interpretation also provides a coherent account of our experience of being drawn toward the future actualization of unforeseen possibilities. As noted above (p. 163), when Ernst Bloch attributes the pull of the not-yet to matter, he assumes the presence in matter of qualities akin to the intelligence and intention historically associated with God. Preferable to this questionable redefinition is a world view which grounds the urge to actualize unforeseen possibilities in the creative energizing of the Spirit who permeates all existence, relates past, present, and future, and seeks among men and women the fullest realization of value.

Realism compels the recognition of the presence in human existence of many factors that cannot be neatly reconciled with faith in God. Some of these are integrally related to intimations of transcendence traced above to the divine presence. The mystery we confront is often fearsome. Human dependence involves not only support for life but the threat of nothingness. All of us face the dangers of accident, disease, infirmity, and war. For millions poverty, meaninglessness, and estrangement from their fellows are agonizing realities. Many persons confront the future in dread, not hope. Death is a certainty for everyone. How can experiences like these be harmonized with belief in a God who cares?

With data like these in mind, Antony Flew has incisively criticized theism for changing the meaning of qualities like goodness and love in order to continue to assert them of God. Though the human father of a child stricken with cancer will do everything in his power to find a cure, there is no evidence that God does anything to arrest the disease. So the theist declares that divine and human love must be understood differently. When the meaning of words can be changed in this way according to convenience, asks Flew, what kind of event could ever falsify or "count against" the assertion that God loves mankind? [18] The theist's frank answer might well be: Any event like the child's cancer, suffering unrelated to value fulfillment, or natural catastrophes which destroy life and thwart human hopes. But what Flew forgets is that no single event could count *decisively* against the affirmations of faith. The verdict would need to be based on all the available evidence, positive and negative, taken as a whole.

Full recognition would then have to be given to the bearing on the causation of human suffering of circumstances like these: (a) Human life would be impossible without a reliably functioning natural order, though hardship may result if it is even inadvertently violated. (2) The social solidarity or interdependence of human beings enables us to benefit immeasurably from the contributions of others, but it also exposes us to the danger of suffering from their carelessness or cruelty. (3) At least a limited degree of free-

[18] Flew and MacIntyre (eds.), *New Essays in Philosophical Theology,* pp. 96-97.

dom is necessary if men and women are to become true persons, but freedom may be thoughtlessly or maliciously misused, inflicting widespread damage and thwarting the fulfillment of life. A degree of freedom may extend to the subhuman order. (4) We may conceive of God himself as sharing deeply in the anguish and pain of existence, yet keeping men and women in his unconquerable love and through suffering ultimately fulfilling his ends. Moreover, if belief in God is rejected another problem arises which is at least as difficult for the atheist as the reality of evil is for the theist—the problem of good. If the cosmos is ultimately indifferent, irrational, and devoid of meaning, how are we to understand the emergence of real values like the pursuit and attainment of truth, the creation and enjoyment of beauty, and the strength of self-forgetful love? Careful discussion here of issues like these would take us too far afield.[19] However, these brief comments may suffice to indicate that in the light of all the data available the theistic position may justly claim to provide the soundest interpretation of our human situation.

Other questions arise regarding the wisdom of interpreting intimations of transcendence in human life in terms of a personal God. If God is purposive, conscious intelligence, and if he desires communion with finite persons, why does he not find ways of making himself known more clearly? Why is he so frequently present only incognito? Here at least three things may be said. First, in an area as vast, complex, and mysterious as our relation to ultimate reality, there is far greater room for misunderstanding and error on the part of the human knower than in the special sciences. Secondly, God as understood in these pages does not coerce his worshipers, but in seeking them for fellowship with himself allows them freedom to resist; without such freedom truly

---

[19] For further discussion of these problems, see my *God in an Age of Atheism,* pp. 179-90.

interpersonal communion would be impossible. Finally, there are positive factors in our experience that are best understood on the personal plane. The questions that rise within us regarding our identity, our values, and our goals, as well as the frequently experienced awareness of being addressed, claimed, or entrusted from some extra-human source, make more sense if they are referred to the God here affirmed than if they are ascribed either to an unknowing cosmos or to the pressures of human society. It is worth noting also that God conceived according to the analogy of human personality, though infinitely greater, offers a better understanding than any purely naturalistic hypothesis of the conjunction in the ultimately real of being and becoming—one of the age-old problems of metaphysics.

With this sampling of pertinent issues, we conclude that belief in God as the ground of our experiences of transcendence can without serious contradiction be woven into a pattern with our other experiences and beliefs, and thus become the basis for a sound understanding of the mutually supportive connections within one whole of reality.

2. *Does referring our experience of the transcendent to divine activity illuminate human existence and help to make it intelligible?* This question overlaps on the preceding one. But whereas we inquired before whether harmonious connections could be found between belief in the independent reality of God and other human experiences and beliefs, here we are asking how far this belief sheds light on other aspects of life and thought and provides clues to the meaning of the whole. Thus the two criteria complement each other.

Alfred North Whitehead writes:

Religion claims that its concepts, though derived primarily from special experiences, are yet of universal validity, to be supplied by faith to the ordering of all experience. Rational religion appeals to the direct intuition of special occasions, and to the elucidatory power of its concepts for all occasions.[20]

If we look at human life and the world in the light shed by faith in God's creative, reconciling, and liberating activity, and find our experience becoming more perceivable and meaningful in that light, we can reasonably regard this fact as evidence for the truth of our faith.

Such "elucidatory power" may be found in the view which refers our intuitions of transcendence to the activity of God. If the activity on which we depend in our experiences of contingency, limitation, and incompleteness is understood as the dynamic life of God moving toward the fulfillment of his purposes, light is cast on the orientation of our individual lives toward the future, as well as on the evolutionary process as a whole. The intricate interrelationships and the open-ended movement from present attainment to future possibility and from simpler to more complex emergents take on greater significance if seen as supported by the God who is himself on the way.

There is no universally convincing answer to the question of the meaning of human existence. Nevertheless, if a good God is conceived to be at the heart of our search for meaning and also as himself the ultimate answer, light penetrates our darkness, and the way we must travel becomes more clear. This is of course the profound assurance of the Prologue to the Fourth Gospel: "The light shines on in the dark, and the darkness has never mastered it" (John 1:5 NEB). We have noted above (pp. 63, 120-21) Viktor Frankl's conviction, gained amid the seeming hopelessness of imprisonment in Nazi concentration camps, that one can always choose the attitude he will take toward a situation he cannot alter, hence that no one can deprive him of his dignity as a person. Thus

[20] *Religion in the Making* (New York: The Macmillan Co., 1926), p. 32.

196

his existence can never be completely meaningless. That this can be true seems almost incredible from a human point of view. Yet we can grasp at least the possibility if we find at the center of our existence one who is the ultimate ground of meaning and of life itself. The same may be said of our quest for wholeness. To find God active in our experiences of self-transcendence, writes H. Richard Niebuhr, imparts wholeness and rationality to the confusions, joys, and sorrows of personal existence and order to the history of human societies.[21]

Another area in which a theistic understanding of transcendent experience proves illuminating is that of interpersonal relations. If, for example, human beings are conceived as formed in "the image of God" (Gen. 1:26-27), light is shed on our knowledge of one another, our dependence on one another, and our participation in community with one another. If we are all created capable of responding to God, then presumably we have in him a common basis for our knowledge of, and solidarity with, one another. If he is the dynamic process that underlies and interpenetrates our lives, then we are not an accidental collection of windowless monads but an intentional connection of persons whose lives and destinies are inextricably interwoven. We share the same world, and it is not a blind, mechanical world, but one in which intelligent Love is seeking to relate persons to one another in dynamic fellowship grounded in their common relation to him.

To see all things in God enables us also to perceive more clearly our relation to nature. If the physical and biological world is the scene of the dynamic activity of God, interdependence characterizes our natural as well as our social environment, and guarding the life chain becomes not only a means of self-preservation, but a way of cooperating with the purposes of God in crea-

[21] *The Meaning of Revelation* (New York: The Macmillan Co., 1941), p. 80.

tion. The selfish exploitation of natural resources is not merely self-defeating, restricting our own opportunities for enjoyment; it also obstructs the divine intention for future generations and possibly other goals which God may have, unknown to us, for his extra-human creation. Ecological and interpersonal responsibility thus reinforce each other, with the addition of a cosmic dimension.

Our experiences of value also take on greater meaning if they are seen in theistic perspective. In them we confront possibilities and claims that we do not produce but find. But since the appreciation of worth on the human level requires conscious awareness and recognition of norms, if we think of values as grounded ultimately in the divine Spirit in whom we live, move, and have our being, we understand more fully their pull upon us. The ethical imperative, for instance, makes much more sense if it is conceived as the righteous will of God than if it is related only to social expediency. Obversely, though our feelings of guilt when we muffle or disobey the voice of conscience may be interpreted purely in terms of social pressure, they are further illuminated when seen to reflect a broken relationship with him who seeks our highest good.

Considerations like these obviously fall short of demonstrating the truth of the theistic interpretation. Nevertheless, they do show that to regard our awareness of the transcendent as basically experience of God—a God whose reality is prior to, and independent of, our thought of him—sheds important light on widely varied facets of our apprehension of existence.

3. *Does the belief that God is actively present in our experiences of self-transcendence enrich the quality of human life, releasing spiritual energies for responsible participation in society?* When William Temple proposes practical effectiveness and philosophical completeness as criteria for judging the truth of claims to divine revelation, he defines the former as "power . . . to

guide men through the perplexities of life." [22] Similarly, A. E. Taylor holds that a religion is true "just in so far as it achieves the purpose . . . of thoroughly remoulding the self." [23] It is this norm that we now seek to apply to the claims of certain experiences to involve the presence of God incognito.

The test of practical effectiveness would be seriously inadequate if taken alone. There is much empirical evidence to show that constructive guidance for life may be derived from mutually contradictory convictions. Such is the psychological power of faith that highly dubious beliefs may contribute to genuine integrity of character. Nevertheless, the principle proposed deserves inclusion in our criteria. A faith that demonstrates ability to make life more abundant may be presumed to contain important elements of truth. If the standard of practical results is applied in close conjunction with the other criteria and constantly checked by them, it may provide valuable additional guidance. Indeed, we are here concerned with the concrete experience which according to the two norms previously examined is to be harmonized and illuminated. Hence we cannot ignore or treat lightly the bearing on ordinary life of the claim that God is active in the intimations of the transcendent disclosed there.

The awareness of "something there" described by William James (above, p. 96) not only points to a dimension of reality that harmonizes well with other data when we interpret it theistically; it also becomes frequently a channel of spiritual strength. The consciousness of participating in a reality that is fuller and deeper than otherwise known is often accompanied by an influx of "grace" akin to that celebrated by persons who affirm the personal presence of God in their lives. Viktor Frankl's accounts of life

[22] John Baillie, and Hugh Martin (eds.), *Revelation* (London: Macmillan & Co., 1937), p. 122.
[23] *The Faith of a Moralist* (London: Macmillan & Co., 1930), II, 81.

in the Nazi concentration camps of the nineteen-forties reveal a real correlation of active religious belief with the capacity for facing the harshness of daily existence with some sense of meaning and some degree of courage and hope. Countless people have likewise discovered amid the routine and uncertainty of ordinary existence that direction becomes clearer and purpose more firm as they seek to relate their lives harmoniously to the inclusive purposes of God.

Interpretation of our spiritual environment in terms of the divine presence also opens the way to the healing of the alienations so characteristic of our time—estrangement from ourselves, from other persons, and from existence itself. To see our lives as grounded ultimately in God and supported by his reconciling, unifying love may empower us to turn from pursuit of our fragmented private interests to become whole persons at home in our social and cosmic environments.

This relationship has profoundly constructive as well as restorative significance. The experience of innumerable men and women shows that faith in God heightens their insights, so that they see things differently; deepens their sense of responsibility; enlarges and strengthens their commitments; and releases new energies, enabling them to assume and carry out new tasks. It is impossible to gainsay the transforming power of religious convictions and an experienced relation to God evidenced in Martin Luther King, Jr., Daniel Berrigan, and others who have attributed to more-than-human resources the confidence and courage with which they have faced opposition, imprisonment, and even death.

It must be freely admitted that the lives of many nontheistic humanists also exhibit great strength of character and self-forgetful dedication to humanitarian goals. By contrast, many professing Christians who speak piously of their salvation through Jesus Christ give little evidence either of ability to handle their own conflicts or of genuine concern for the well-being of other persons in society. Obviously the evidence does not fit into a neat, unambiguous pattern, and again we need to seek the best interpretation of the data as a whole. The burning zeal of the socially-minded atheist may spring wholly from his own sensitivity to human suffering. But conceivably he may be responding to something deeply rooted in reality which binds him to his fellows, without recognizing its ultimacy. The pathetic hollowness of faith of the self-centered believer may signify the absence of any objective ground. But possibly it can be more soundly understood as the result of human limitations, misused freedom, or sinful distortion. The extra-human resources for dynamic living by persons in society may be real enough, yet prevented from exerting their transforming influence by human obstructions. No decision on these alternatives can hope to win general assent.

There is, however, a kind of empirical verification of the theistic option. As we have seen (above, pp. 112-15), many Marxists and other humanists join with Christians in affirming a self-transcending quality in human existence. Aware of our incompleteness, we feel impelled to seek the fulfillment of our unrealized possibilities. In this process we become aware of our relation to an environing reality on which we depend: it gives us life, sustains us, and challenges us to actualize our potential. Effective struggle toward greater completeness depends not only on our own efforts, but on this complex other which constantly impinges on us. Indeed, a positive relation to this other is a condition of our fullest self-realization. We cannot become fully human apart from such a relationship. Without it we become ingrown and stunted; with it the way is open to largest growth. We seem to confront here something structural in reality, a creative process that precedes, underlies, calls forth, and responds supportively to our striving for worthy ends.

Looking back over the territory just covered, we can note a convergence of the several lines of investigation. They lead toward the conclusion that the intimations of transcendence encountered in experience disclose a genuine relationship of men and women to divine reality, a reality best conceived as the dynamic, personal love that sustains and permeates the whole of our existence.

This judgment will not win universal assent. It does not neatly remove all difficulties. It demands further critical exploration. But it is supported by a wide variety of weighty evidence. It can be related coherently to knowledge derived from other sources and to our experience as a whole. It sheds important light on human existence in many of its aspects, making it more intelligible. It enriches human life, releases strength for responsible meeting of its demands, and contributes to our fullest realization of value. It therefore merits the respect of all who seek truth concerning the ultimate mysteries.

We need not search for God as though he were somewhere else. He is everywhere. In our daily experiences of depth, dependence, meaning, personal and social responsibility, and outreach toward the future in hope we are already in his presence. If we at least hold ourselves open to the possibility that this is true, and act upon it, we may discover that God is no longer absent or even present incognito, but a living reality in our own experience here and now.

INDEX OF PERSONS

203

God Incognito

INDEX OF SUBJECTS